Art Blakey's Jazz Messages

JOHN RAMSAY

drum transcriptions by **JOHN RAMSAY**

text edited by **PAUL SIEGEL**

music edited by **DAN THRESS**

PUBLISHED BY **ALFRED MUSIC PUBLISHING CO., INC.**

©1994, 2009 MANHATTAN MUSIC, INC.

ALL RIGHTS CONTROLLED AND ADMINISTERED BY ALFRED MUSIC PUBLISHING CO., INC.
ALL RIGHTS RESERVED. INTERNATIONAL COPYRIGHT SECURED. MADE IN USA

ALL FRANCIS WOLFF PHOTOGRAPHY © 1994 BY MOSAIC IMAGES.

ISBN-10: 0-7604-0009-1 (BOOK & CD)
ISBN-13: 978-0-7604-0009-8 (BOOK & CD)

Dedicated in loving memory to

ABDULLAH IBN BUHAINA
a.k.a.

ART BLAKEY

BOOK DESIGN & MUSIC ENGRAVING

WILLIAM R. BRINKLEY & ASSOCIATES
SOMERVILLE, MA

COVER DESIGN

JACK WALTRIP

PRODUCTION COORDINATOR

DAN THRESS

AUDIO TAPE

PRODUCED BY

JOHN RAMSAY *AND* JON HAZILLA *AT*
PETER KONTRIMAS' PBS Studio
WESTWOOD, MA

PHOTOGRAPHY

FRANCIS WOLFF
COURTESY OF CHARLIE LOURIE, Mosaic Images
EXCEPT WHERE NOTED

FOREWORD

"You never see an armored car following a hearse." So spoke the great Art Blakey when attempting to bolster the flagging confidence of young, weak, and less concerned musicians (we were always around in case this sort of verbal inspiration was proffered — it often was). So interjected Abdullah Ibn Buhaina as high priest of mythology at the most recent funeral for jazz in explaining why the meat hook of commercialism would not slice into his soul sliding him, embarrassed from the stage as jazz master to the spiritual freezer of publicly acclaimed puppet (it had snared so many of his even more-renowned colleagues). This is what Art Blakey said when convincing again his many enthralled audiences that the hot sound of a band swinging would proudly resound no matter how deteriorated the contemporary social virtues.

Mikell's Night Spot early eighties: people packed, unabashedly exhibiting the love and respect reserved solely for the most venerated of long- standing warriors. Art Blakey at the helm of a band of young would-bes, perched on the orange throne of a drum set, head cocked heavenward, mouth open in wonder, eyes flashing in the act of creating, listening as he hammers the supremacy of swinging out into the still, smoky night air. The young not believing their good fortune — sharing the bandstand with the living embodiment of what they want to dedicate their lives to. They too thought the funeral for jazz was last week — they read it in all the magazines — but here is a priest of it, alive and willing to teach by playing with them — to give himself up to them and those listening. Why should he? "From the creator, to the artist, to you." So spoke the great Art Blakey in explaining why he played every gig like it was his first and last.

He was the greatest man most of us will ever know. Capable of doing more of "everything" than anyone you ever heard of. Folks used to say, "On the eighth day, God created Art Blakey." He was just made of something else, different from us (mere) mortals. It was the integrity and soul of the man; he was unshakable, with an indestructible belief in soul and intelligence melded into an inseparable one through jazz music that inspired him to stay on the road shaping excellent band after band long after most of his generation and younger had faded and curled like bad, old and loud wall paper. He loved this music and the musicians that played it and they loved him back even under the most adverse circumstances (of which there were many).

He loved to swing and help others to swing. That's what he did full out, all night long — daytime too … all the time!! You thought it wasn't hard for him to live with this heroic intensity because, well, he lived jazz music and was at all times totally himself, unique, inimitable, bred by Mrs. Blakey to too-hard work. He could even tell a lie with such integrity as to have you agreeing — even when it was on you. He was a great storyteller who loved and knew intimately all sorts of people from criminals to the judges. Yes, and they loved him because he was a magician and everyone loves magic. His was the magic of powerful rhythms. Yes, he was a magician whose sleight-of-hand tricks converted a trap set from cow skin, wood, and sheet metal to the many creaks, moans, groans, hollers, and whistles of nature of a quiet then stormy night. "Never let one hand know what the other is doing." So spoke Bu in describing the execution of some impossible to play polyrhythm. So he spoke as Merlin in the process of casting a spell to unify contrasting rhythms into harmonious tapestry of swinging sound. He was a drummer, could control the sound of a band like you wouldn't believe, but would give you chances to control it — if you wanted to, if you could, or if you were trying. Because he was patient; would let you learn how to play at his expense. But now, if you were bullshitting, "here comes this bass drum right up your ass to make you play something — mother. . . . . . !!" He was no saint, but a hero bred to battle. Possessed of an inborn fire that could not be doused. A hot, passionate combination of fury, calm, greed, generosity, intelligence, and soul, yes, that is what he was most of all — unconquerable.

You might have heard that he could do more of "everything" than anyone else (people like to talk about things like that — and maybe it was true) but did I mention that really, he loved to swing and help others to swing too? Well, that is the truth — about him anyway.

Wynton Marsalis, May 1994

CONTENTS

AUDIO EXAMPLES

1   OPENING DRUM SOLO   2:12

2   INTRODUCTION TO AUDIO EXAMPLES   0:38

3   CHAPTER 1   TIMEKEEPING LICKS
Examples 1a–7d   35:55
minus 2e, 2f, 3c, 3d, 3e3, 3l, 3m, and 7d

4   CHAPTER 2   TIMEKEEPING TRANSCRIPTIONS
Humph (fast version only)   3:29

5   CHAPTER 3   SOLO LICKS
Examples 1a–6e   29:29
minus 1k, 1m, and 3e

6   CHAPTER 4   SOLO TRANSCRIPTIONS
This I Dig of You (fast version only)   1:20

A NOTE ON THE LANGUAGE USED IN THIS BOOK

In an effort to capture the spirit of the musicians who were generous enough to allow themselves to be interviewed for this book, and also to communicate the true spirit of Art Blakey, we have retained most of the language of the original interviews, including occasional profanity and the use of vernacular expressions. Although we made certain alterations (since we would hope that drummers of all ages will enjoy this book) we felt that the basic intention would be better served by changing the original language as little as possible.

The Publishers

ACKNOWLEDGMENTS

For Julia, who provided love and support and a beautiful tropical paradise to write in, and without whom this book could not have been completed.

For my children Corey, Shaka, Niko and Evan Ramsay; my sisters Joy and Bobby, and my father Percy; and for Art Blakey's children Gwendolyn, Art Jr. and Evelyn Blakey; Gamal, Sakeena, Takashi, Kenji and Akira Buhaina; Ann Arnold Blakey, Yawu Miller and the whole family.

A special thanks to all the Jazz Messengers who contributed to this book, and especially Wynton Marsalis, for his loving Foreword.

Thanks to the other spirit of the drums, Lenny Nelson — you're an inspiration for all drummers. Yeah, Universal Dexterity!

Special Thanks to Javon Jackson for hookin' me up with "the cats." And to my brother Billy Pierce.

Thanks to Paul Siegel, Bob Weiner, Kim Plainfield, Bill Brinkley, John Riley, Alan Dawson, Sandy Feldstein, Charlie Banacos, Tommy Campbell, Louis LoCicero and Don Sickler; Andy Zildjian and Steve Oksenuk at Sabian Cymbals, Vic Firth and Carol Calato; Larry Monroe, Warrick Carter, Lee Berk, Dean Anderson, and the Berklee College of Music percussion faculty.

Thanks to Hannes Giese for the discography in his book *Art Blakey Sein Leben, Seine Musik, Seine Schallplatten (His Love, His Music, His Records)*, published in Germany by Oreos books.

John P Ramsay

ABOUT THE AUTHOR

Drummer, recording artist, author, educator, clinician — these are all words which describe John Ramsay.

John is featured with the Art Blakey and the Jazz Messengers Big Band on a recent Blue Note Records Compact Disc entitled *The History of Art Blakey and the Jazz Messengers*, and the 1980 Timeless release *Art Blakey and the Jazz Messengers Big Band Live in Montreux and North Sea*.

In addition to these recordings, John can be heard on the 1993 debut CD release for tenor saxophonist Les Arbuckle *No More No Les*, featuring Kenny Barron and Cecil McBee for Audioquest Records, and on Lionel Hampton saxophonist Andy McGhee's first release as a leader, *Could It Be*, with Ray Santisi and Joe Cohn.

John has been heavily involved in teaching at Berklee College of Music in Boston where he has taught for the past twelve Years. He has participated in many *Berklee on the Road* activities including jazz clinics in Italy, Poland, Japan and in the United States in Santa Fe and Los Angeles. He has also performed at Jazz Educators seminars in St. Louis, New Orleans, Miami and Boston.

Aside from his membership in the Jazz Messengers Big Band, John served as road manager and occasional drum sub in the Jazz Messengers Sextet. John's close personal relationship with Art lasted until Art's death in 1990.

Born in Northampton, Massachusetts, John grew up in the 1960's playing the popular music of the period. His musical direction was permanently altered with the advent of Jazz/Rock fusion and with the arrival of Max Roach to his alma mater, the University of Massachusetts at Amherst. It was during this period of study and with the guidance of Max Roach that John first became aware of the great American art form of jazz. This led to a five- year period of study with master drummer/educator Alan Dawson, who John credits with giving him the well-rounded skills necessary to survive in the music business. John also studied with Ed Soph and Bob Moses, and continues to study and learn by taking occasional lessons and transcribing the recordings of great drummers of our time. John says: "That's one of the wonderful things about music and drumming, it's a lifetime endeavor. One can always learn something new."

In addition to the Art Blakey and the Jazz Messengers Big Band, which included Wynton and Branford Marsalis, Kevin and Robin Eubanks, James Williams and Bill Pierce, John has performed with Sonny Stitt, James Moody, Terence Blanchard, Wallace Roney, Donald Harrison, Donald Brown, Kenny Barron, Cecil McBee, Eartha Kitt, Gregory Hines, John Hicks, Walter Booker and The Clifford Jordan Big Band. John endorses Sabian Cymbals and Regal Tip/Calato drumsticks and brushes.

INTRODUCTION

In January of 1980 I was playing in Waitsfield, Vermont, with Sonny Stitt. It was there that I met Art Blakey's son, Gamal Buhaina. I was surprised (and flattered) when Gamal told me my playing reminded him of his father's. I was even more surprised when several months later he called and said that Art was forming a Big Band with two drummers and he wanted me to audition.

I made the audition and became the drummer with Art Blakey and the Jazz Messengers Big Band (see album of the same name, Timeless Records no. SJP 150). Art and I both played drums at the same time. Art would say, "If two horn players can play together, then two drummers can play together."

This began a two-and-a-half year affiliation with Art Blakey and various editions of Jazz Messengers from 1980 to 1982, beginning with my role as drummer for the Big Band, and later as road manager for the regular Jazz Messengers Sextet.

As road manager, I played a number of different roles, acting as stage manager, soundman, drumtech, rehearsal drummer, substitute drummer, record producer, driver, accountant, master of ceremonies, and more. During my time with the Jazz Messengers I completed nine tours of Europe, one tour of Japan, trips to the West Indies and Iceland, and several cross-country tours of the United States.

It was during these tours that I had the opportunity to hear and see Art play, sometimes six and seven nights a week. Art liked to work and whenever possible would tour forty to fifty weeks a year.

My time spent with the Jazz Messengers became the inspiration for writing this book. Before his death in 1990, Art and I spoke often about writing a book about his drumming. However, when I left the Messengers in 1982, I came to Berklee College to teach and kept delaying the project. Over the years I've included in my teaching much of what I learned from Art, spiritually as well as musically. Many of my students and peers have encouraged me to write this book and suggested that I'm perhaps more qualified to do so than anyone else because of the insight that I have into Art's sticking and Art's voicings on the drumset. I saw Art play most of the ideas in this book on many occasions; therefore, when I hear the recordings I have a vivid picture of his execution.

A BOUT THE BOOK

Timekeeping Licks

At Berklee, one of the areas I teach is timekeeping. In recent years I have come to question the more traditional ways in which coordination/timekeeping has been taught (e.g., the use of syncopation). Most studies of this type are rather "notey" and in my opinion don't accurately reflect the way a jazz drummer "comps" or keeps time. It is my hope that in this section drummers will gain insight into how one of the greatest of all jazz drummers kept time behind the soloists he accompanied.

I urge you to consult the recordings listed for all the examples to get the subtleties and nuances that are more difficult to notate, and to hear the interplay between the drums and the other instruments. Listen to the way the drums and the piano "comp" together and how the rhythm section works as a unit.

This section was intended to be a partial vocabulary of timekeeping "licks" or motifs, and is by no means meant to be all-inclusive.

Timekeeping Transcriptions

In this section you will be able to see and hear longer examples of Art's timekeeping style. I suggest consulting the recordings and listening for how the other instruments may have influenced what Art played.

There are transcriptions from 1947 ("Humph") to 1981 ("Cheryl"). When you compare the two, I think you can hear how Art's style grew and evolved over the years. The 1947 recording shows a style more like that of the 1930's and 1940's, whereas the 1981 recording is like that of the be-bop and hard-bop style that Art helped create.

Solo Licks

This section, like the Timekeeping Licks section, can be used as a catalogue of figures to be added to the drummer's vocabulary of solo ideas. One of the things I do in my teaching is to have students solo over the form of a standard tune (credit must be given to Alan Dawson for this exercise). Many students have commented that they did not know what to play for solos. This section can provide some ideas as to what to play for solos. However, I would caution against playing a solo that consists solely of licks. I suggest trying to combine licks with melodic ideas and more spontaneous creation, with the aim always being to create *musical* solos. Again, I urge you to consult the recordings listed here and listen for the subtleties.

Frequently, when Art played solos he hit the drums very forcefully. This had a lot to do with the sound he got from the instrument. He would often switch to matched grip playing with the butt of the stick in the left hand. He did this particularly when playing things on the tom-toms, as on "A Night in Tunisia."

Art used many of these licks not only during solos, but also as fills or embellishments during timekeeping or when playing the heads of tunes. Therefore, you should not limit these ideas strictly to solos.

Solo Transcriptions

This section, in conjunction with the recordings, provides the opportunity to see how Art uses the licks from the previous section, and to hear more extended solos. Some of these solos are transcriptions of trading "fours" or "eights" and others are more extended transcriptions of entire choruses, some are drum introductions. You can extract ideas from these extended solos and learn them in part, or learn the entire transcription.

As with the previous sections, I strongly suggest consulting the recordings.

Heads

Art has been called the most musical and orchestral of drummers. In this section I hope to show how he would orchestrate a piece of music by shaping it and embellishing it from the drumset by using dynamics, and by filling in between phrases; he seemed to breathe life into anyone's composition.

Many of Art's patented licks and figures can be found throughout this section showing how he got the most out of his vocabulary and how he integrated what he played into timekeeping as well as soloing.

Of particular interest is the tune "Free for All" and how Art sets up a polyrhythmic feeling of three within four. Again, listen to the original recordings.

Notebooks

The original source of the ideas for this book, which began in 1980, were pocket notebooks I kept during my tenure as road manager. The examples in this section are from those notebooks, and are presented exactly as written over ten years ago.

Interviews

The interviews in this section are longer than the anecdotal "Jazz Messages" that appear in the book. They are also more candid and personal, and a great deal of love and admiration for Art comes through. I also recommend a new book, *52nd St. Beat* (1994; published by Jamey Abersold Jazz, Inc.) by my Berklee colleague Joe Hunt, which contains some very valuable quotes from Art Blakey.

About the References

When I began this book my idea was to play and write down every lick I learned from watching and hearing Art Blakey. I began by doing just that; I got out a tape recorder and went through everything I could remember. In the course of doing that, questions arose as to whether or not I was playing things exactly the way Art had. It was then that I decided to consult his recordings to verify what I had written. This confirmed some things and shed new light on others. Originally there were references to over forty different albums and CDs. To simplify matters and to make these references more accessible to the reader I went back over everything and was able to find most of the examples on one three-set Blue Note CD package, *The History of Art Blakey and the Jazz Messengers*, CDP 7 97190 2. It is an excellent compilation of many of Art's recordings and well worth the price.

About the Audio Examples

As I mentioned above, while writing this book, I consulted Art Blakey's recordings to verify the accuracy of the examples.

The publishers and I had hoped to obtain licensing from the record companies to include excerpts of the actual recordings referred to in the book. This proved to be too infeasible; therefore, we decided that I would record the examples myself. Although I had some reservations about imiting Art, once the recordings were made I was pleased with the results.

Through my teaching I have discovered that people learn in three basic ways: visually, kinesthetically (through movement), and aurally. The audio portion of this book is an important addition for those of us who have a propensity toward the aural, "hearing" way of learning.

ART BLAKEY

by YAWU MILLER

With a career spanning six decades, Art Blakey looms as one of the giants of jazz music. Born in Pittsburgh, Pa. in 1919, Blakey grew up with a devout Seventh Day Adventist foster family and developed his chops playing piano for the church choir. He played with different jazz bands in Pittsburgh in the early thirties, until a young pianist named Errol Garner took his gig at the Democratic Club. "Man that cat was in patches, but he upset the joint," Art recalled. Art told reporters he was then forced, at gunpoint (!), to play the drums. While continuing to perform, Art worked as a valet to the legendary drummer Chick Webb, under whose mentorship he was able to develop his own style. Art fondly recalled drum battles between Webb and Gene Krupa in New York's Savoy Ballroom.

In 1937, Art returned to Pittsburgh to form his own band. In that same year, pianist Mary Lou Williams joined the band, which was then billed under her name. In 1939, Art hit the big time with a gig in Fletcher Henderson's big band, staying on for three years. After a one-year stint at Boston's Tic Toc club with his own band, he signed on with Billy Eckstine's legendary big band, where he joined forces with be-bop giants including Sarah Vaughan, Charlie Parker and Dizzy Gillespie. It was during his work in Eckstine's band that Art gained recognition for his individual style.

In 1948, Art told reporters he had visited Africa, studying rhythms and Islam. Upon his return to the States, he assumed the name Abdulla Ibn Buhaina. Also at this time, Art assembled a seventeen-piece big band he called the Jazz Messengers — the name he continued to use for his band for over forty years. In 1949, Art took a brief gig with Buddy Defranco before forming the Jazz Messengers with pianist Horace Silver. Altoist Lou Donaldson, trumpeter Kenny Dorham, and bassist Gene Ramey filled out the quintet in 1953.

The early years of the Jazz Messengers were characterized by Art's indomitable energy, Silver's funky compositions, and a revolving door of talented horn men including tenor giant Johnny Griffin, altoist Jackie McClean, tenor player Hank Mobley and legendary trumpeter Clifford Brown, with whom Art recorded a *Live at Birdland* album. During this time, Art often collaborated with his close friend Thelonius Monk. The cooperative idea petered out, and when Silver left the band in 1957, Art began to develop a distinctive sound for the Jazz Messengers (exemplified by "A Night in Tunisia"). When Benny Golson enlisted his help in 1958, the Jazz Messengers gained many of the signature songs which persisted through the last years of the band including Golson's "Along Came Betty" and "Blues March." Golson brought on board fellow Philadelphians Lee Morgan and Bobby Timmons who composed "Moanin'," one of the Messengers' most famous signature tunes; bassist Jymie Merritt rounded out the quintet. The Jazz Messengers also gained international recognition at this point, touring Europe and North Africa.

In 1959, Wayne Shorter replaced Golson on the tenor and took up the mantle of musical director; Shorter proved to be a capable arranger and a prolific songwriter. European tours were becoming routine, and in 1960 the Messengers became the first American jazz band to perform in Japan. At the Tokyo airport, the Messengers were greeted by hundreds of fans as their music was played over the loudspeaker. Over the years, Art enjoyed celebrity status in Japan, making more than forty trips and numerous recordings there.

During this period the Messengers also recorded frequently for the Riverside label, and also with Blue Note (releasing about thirty albums on the latter). An important addition to the band was made in 1961, when trombonist Curtis Fuller signed on. (Like many Messengers, Fuller returned to the band on numerous occasions over the years.) By 1962, Morgan and Timmons had been replaced by Freddie Hubbard and Cedar Walton. Other notable additions in the sixties included Chuck Mangione, Keith Jarrett, Reggie Workman, Lucky Thompson, John Hicks, Bill Hardman, Ronnie Matthews, JoAnne Brackeen and Julien Priester.

During the virtual jazz drought of the seventies, Blakey continued his non-stop touring and released several records, maintaining the tradition of "straight-ahead jazz." Moving into the early eighties, Art and Messengers Bobby Watson (alto), Billy Pierce (tenor), James Williams (piano) and upstart trumpeter Wynton Marsalis led the charge in the revival in popularity of straight-ahead jazz. With bassist Charles Fambrough completing the quintet, this band was considered one of the best since the sixties.

Other Messengers in the eighties included trumpeters Wallace Roney and Terence Blanchard, pianists Mulgrew Miller and Donald Brown, bassists Peter Washington and Lonnie Plaxico and alternate drummer John Ramsay. Art died at age seventy-one after over fifty years of performing. With scores of Messengers still active, the music lives on.

Jazz Drumming Nuances

Feathering

Art Blakey, like most jazz drummers, usually played quarter-notes on the bass drum very softly. Jazz drummers refer to this as "feathering," which should be felt rather than heard.

Many of the examples in the book indicate quarter-notes on the bass drum, and 2 & 4 on the hi-hat. Unless otherwise notated, this feathering technique should be used.

Ride Cymbal Interpretation

I have used a variety of ride cymbal notations, e.g.

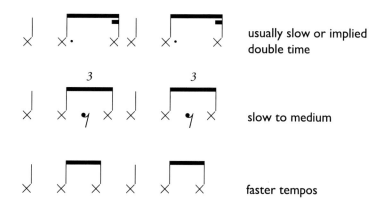

It is recommended that you take these as a guide and not as a rule. The actual interpretation of the ride pattern will change with the tempo of a given piece. The following can serve as a guide.

I urge you to consult the recordings listed and decide for yourself which cymbal interpretation Art actually played.

KEY

CYMBALS

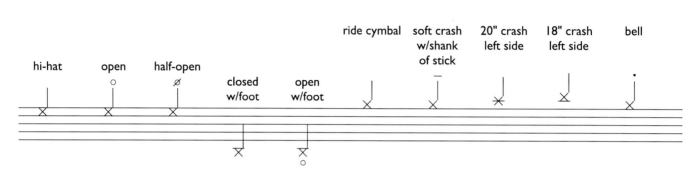

hi-hat — open — half-open — closed w/foot — open w/foot — ride cymbal — soft crash w/shank of stick — 20" crash left side — 18" crash left side — bell

BASS/SNARE

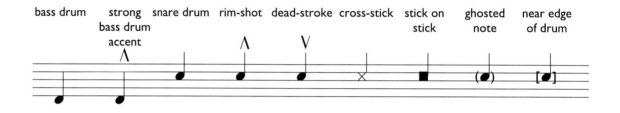

bass drum — strong bass drum accent — snare drum — rim-shot — dead-stroke — cross-stick — stick on stick — ghosted note — near edge of drum

TOMS

CHAPTER 3

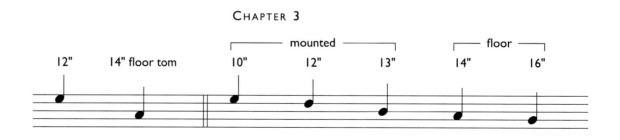

12" — 14" floor tom — mounted — 10" — 12" — 13" — floor — 14" — 16"

1 Opening Drum Solo

COMPING IDEAS

Ex. 1a Art's favorite comping lick

REFERENCE **"Justice"** 4th bar of trumpet solo

CD: *The History of Art Blakey and the Jazz Messengers*
Blue Note CPD 7 97190 2

Be sure to play a rim shot on beat one of the last bar.

Ex. 1b

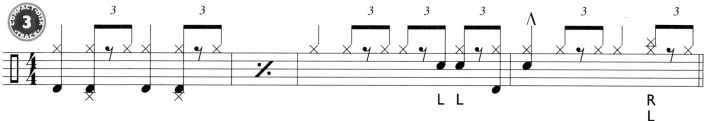

REFERENCE **"Lester Left Town"** 3rd bar of the bridge
(19th bar) on 1st chorus

album: *The Big Beat*
Blue Note BST 84029

"Little Melonae" 8th bar of 2nd A of the head

album: *Art Blakey, the Jazz Messenger*
Columbia CL 1040

"BLAKEY TRIPLETS"

Ex. 1c Practice this slowly and evenly, and be sure to accent.

REFERENCE **"The Egyptian"** intro

album: *Indestructible*
Blue Note 84193

Example **1c**, moving around the drums

REFERENCE **"The Egyptian"** intro

album: *Indestructible*
Blue Note 84193

Ex. 1d Be sure to get a full cross-stick sound. Experiment with different stick positions to find that "sweet spot."

REFERENCE   **"Doodlin'"** 12th bar of the 2nd A section

album: *The Big Beat* Blue Note BST 84029 or

CD: *The History of Art Blakey and the Jazz Messengers*
Blue Note CDP 7 97190 2

Ex. 1e This is a very challenging figure; practice it very slowly at first and then try it up to the tempo of the recording (♩=186).

REFERENCE   **"This is for Albert"** introduction and head

album: *Caravan*
Riverside Records RM 438

MORE COMPING IDEAS

Ex. 1f Play the small tom with the butt end of the stick; use matched grip.

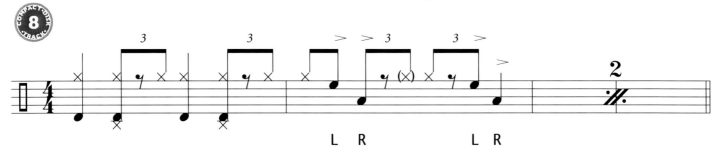

REFERENCE   **"Lester Left Town"** 16th bar of the trumpet solo

album: *The Big Beat*
Blue Note BST 84029 or

CD: *The History of Art Blakey and the Jazz Messengers*
Blue Note CDP 7 97190 2

Ex. 1g This example is transcribed from Art's first recording for Blue Note in 1947. It is of interest because of the phrasing between the snare drum and the bass drum and how they punctuate what the soloist plays. Once again, feather the bass drum on all four beats unless notated otherwise.

REFERENCE **"The Thin Man"** bars 13-32 of the trumpet solo
album: *New Sounds*
Blue Note CD: CDP 844362 or

CD: *The History of Art Blakey and the Jazz Messengers*
Blue Note CDP 7 97190 2

Art's Jazz Messages

Mulgrew Miller told me that one night when the band seemed to lack energy Art called the group together in the dressing room during the break and told them, "If you mother. . . . . . don't play I'm gonna run over you like a Sherman tank!"

One time while playing a shuffle with the Big Band at the beginning of the bass solo Art looked over at me and said, "Keep it right there (meaning the shuffle beat) no matter what he does, keep it right there!"

— John Ramsay

I recall Art telling me "You're gonna' be great in spite of yourself."

Art gave me valuable business advice when he said, "Only the birds sing for free."

— Mulgrew Miller
PIANO; July 1982–September 1986

Ex. 1h This example is usually played at faster tempos.

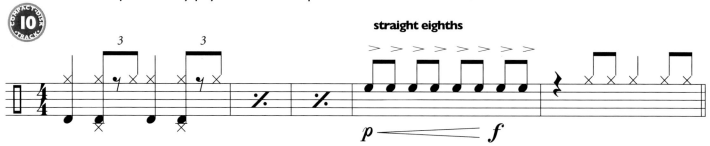

REFERENCE   **"Duck Soup"** 4th bar of piano solo

album: *Oh By the Way*

Timeless Records SJP 165

Ex. 1i Again, practice this very slowly and be sure to subdivide as eighth note triplets.

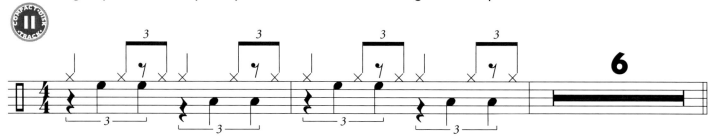

REFERENCE   **"A Night in Tunisia"** bridge of 2nd alto chorus

album: *A Night at Birdland*

Blue Note 1522 vol. 1

Art's Jazz Messages

Once after playing the tune "Moanin'" and trying to run Giant Step-like patterns, Art told me "Let the punishment fit the crime. If you're playing 'Moanin',' play 'Moanin'.' Let the solo develop organically within the context of the composition."

Also in regard to building solos he said, "Rome wasn't built in a day; take time to develop. You can't hit a home run every time." Also, "Take some, leave some. Don't try to play everything you know on every tune."

Art once told me, "It takes five years to build a band."

Art's attitude on the bandstand was that no matter how he felt or what was going on in his life at that time, he was going to get off on the music and enjoy himself. He was going to have total enjoyment.

Art told me "Your greatest asset is your memory."

— *Robert Watson*

ALTO SAXOPHONE; January 1977–August 1981

Art had little chants and comments he would call out from behind the drums designed to encourage and spur on the soloist. Some of those were as follows:

"Act like a fool."

"Get mad."

"Play your instrument."

"Blow your horn."

"Go for it, even if you make a fool of yourself."

— *John Ramsay*

Ex. Ij Art played a lot of notes off the beat (the "ands"); this gave the music a lot of forward momentum.

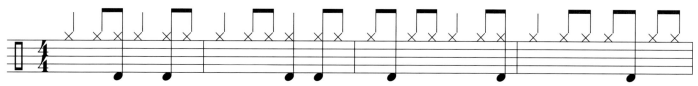

L L R R R R R

Ex. Ik   I find the next two examples of interest because of the way Art used the bass drum.

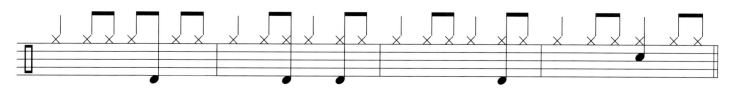

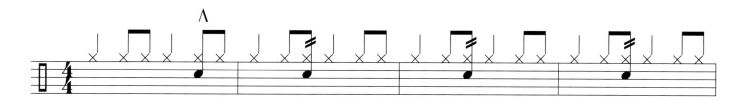

Ex. Il The bass drum sixteenth notes in the last bar are challenging. (The written example is different from the audio example: play the exercise as it appears here.) Buzz the snare drum with the left hand in bars 2, 3, 4 and 6

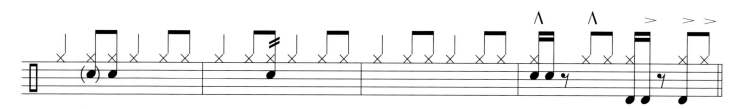

Ex. 2a   Art played this frequently behind piano solos.

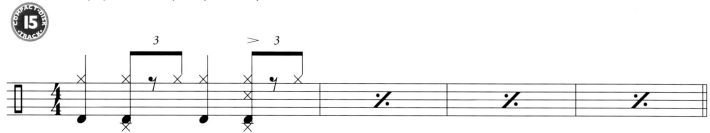

> **REFERENCE**   **"Arabia"** throughout the entire tune
>
> CD: *The History of Art Blakey and the Jazz Messengers*
> Blue Note CDP 7 97190 2

Ex. 2b   This figure has an Afro-Cuban influence.

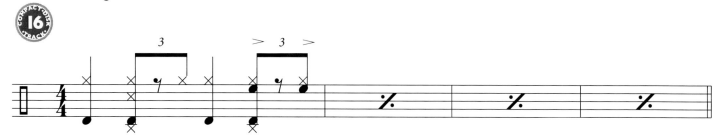

> **REFERENCE**   **"It's Only a Paper Moon"** trombone solo 2nd
> and 3rd chorus
>
> album: *Art Blakey Live at the Renaissance Club*

Ex. 2c   This example is similar to figures **3e1**, **3e2** and **3e3** in this section.

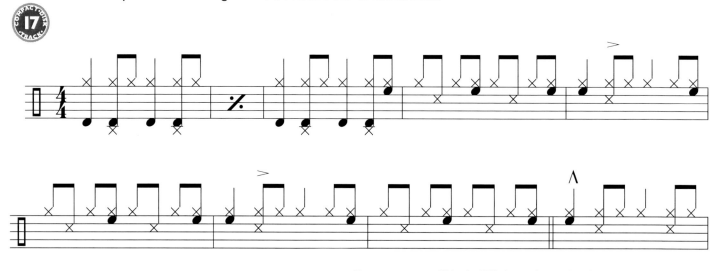

> **REFERENCE**   **"Little T"** throughout the drum solo
>
> CD: *The History of Art Blakey and the Jazz Messengers*
> Blue Note CDP 7 97190 2
>
> **"Are You Real"** 4th drum "fours" during
> trading "fours"
>
> album: *Moanin'*
> Blue Note 4003

DOUBLE PARADIDDLE IDEAS

Art would sometimes employ a double paradiddle, played between the right and left cymbals on the first beat of each double paradiddle, filling in the other notes on the snare drum. The effect of this is a polyrhythm of 3 over (or within) 4.

Ex. 2d

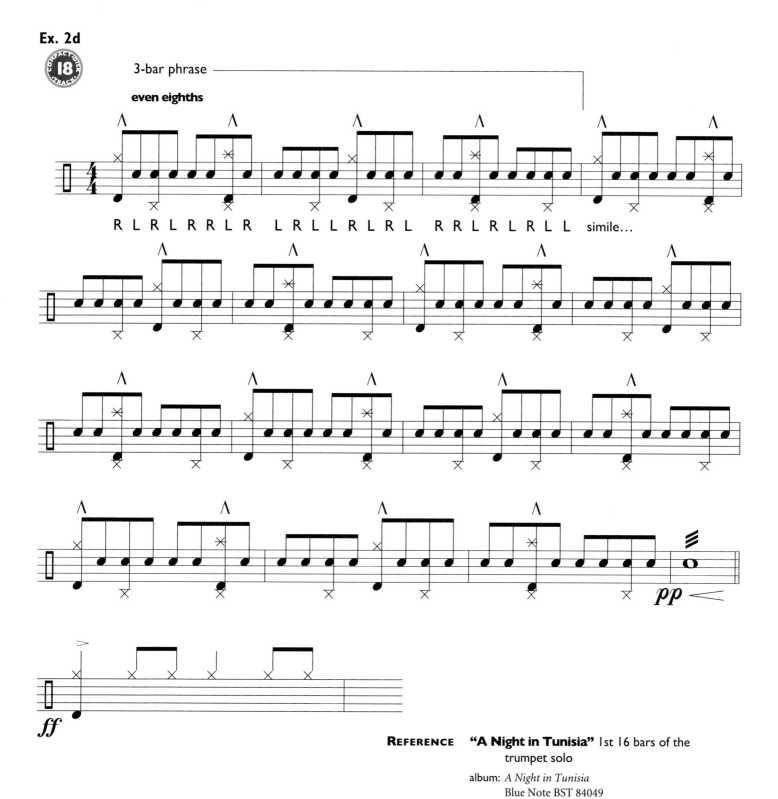

REFERENCE   **"A Night in Tunisia"** 1st 16 bars of the trumpet solo

album: *A Night in Tunisia*
Blue Note BST 84049

Ex. 2e   Another example of the double paradiddle

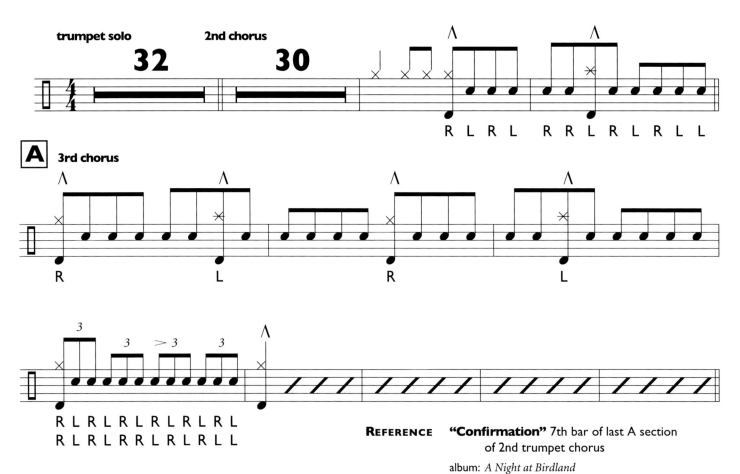

REFERENCE   **"Confirmation"** 7th bar of last A section of 2nd trumpet chorus

album: *A Night at Birdland*
Blue Note BN 1522 vol. 2

Ex. 2f   Double paradiddle optional ending

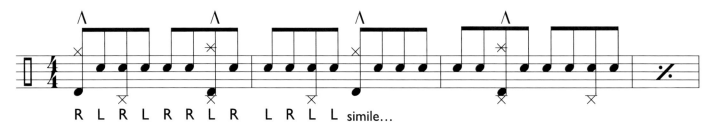

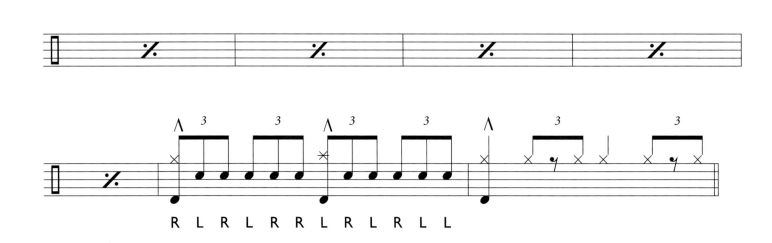

All examples below played with bass drum quarter notes and the hi-hat 2 and 4:

These quarter note triplets create a polyrhythm of 3 over 2. Art would play them most often as a cross-stick pattern (**3c** and **3d**.)

Ex. 3a   or **Ex. 3b**

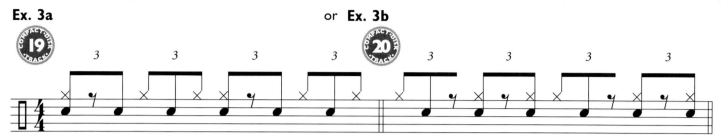

Ex. 3c   or **Ex. 3d**

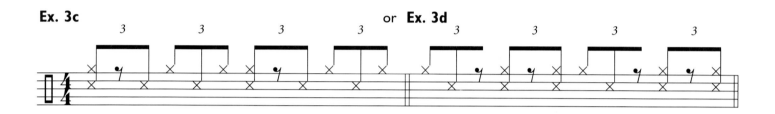

Ex. 3e1 The snare drum cross-stick rhythm creates a half note triplet or a polyrhythm 3 over 4. Try starting on the small tom-tom.

Ex. 3e2 This example is similar to **3e1**. The over-the-bar line effect is very interesting.

REFERENCE   **"Little T"** starting in the 18th bar of the drum solo

CD: *The History of Art Blakey and the Jazz Messengers*
Blue Note CDP 7 97190 2

Ex. 3e3 This example is complex. Practice it very slowly and subdivide with sixteenth notes. Count aloud, saying "1-e-and-a 2-e-and-a" etc. and listen to the original.

REFERENCE   **"Little T"** starting in the 31st bar of drum solo

CD: *The History of Art Blakey and the Jazz Messengers*
Blue Note CDP 7 97190 2

Art's Jazz Messages

James Williams, who played piano with the band for five years and who describes himself as "the astute observer," offered the following:

Art was a master at reading an audience and knowing when to play the "hits" (tunes like "Moanin'," "Blues March," "Along Came Betty" and others.)

Art told me that the bandstand was sacred, that when he (Art) had played with Monk they would open with the spiritual "Abide With Me" and that when the music was right it felt like the bandstand would rise up off the floor.

Art told me to "never let your playing fall below a certain level." Art said "Sometimes you'll play over your head."

I believe that Art led by example.

— *James Williams*
PIANO; October 1977–July 1981

Variations on a theme

Ex. 3f Play the buzz two to three inches from the edge of the drum.

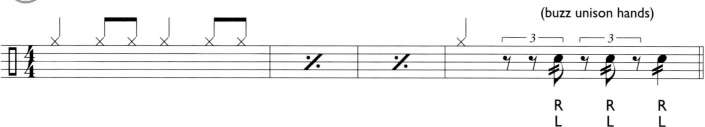

(buzz unison hands)

REFERENCE **"One By One"** 8th bar of A section of head
album: *Oh By the Way*
Timeless Records SJP 165

Ex. 3g Play the left cymbal crash with the butt of the stick (matched grip).

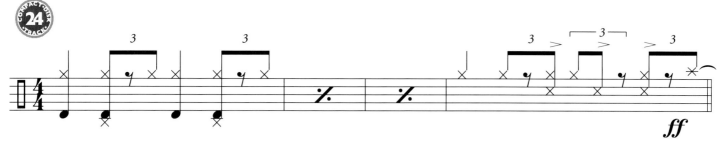

ff

REFERENCE **"Along Came Betty"** 16th bar of trumpet solo
album: *Moanin'*
Blue Note BN 4003

Ex. 3h

REFERENCE **"Along Came Betty"** 3rd and 4th bar of last
A section of trumpet solo
album: *Moanin'*
Blue Note BN 4003

Ex. 3i Art would sometimes set up ensemble figures like this:

(buzz unison hands)

REFERENCE **"The Egyptian"** introduction
album: *Indestructible*
Blue Note 84193 or

CD: *The History of Art Blakey and the Jazz Messengers*
Blue Note CDP 7 97190 2

Ex. 3j   Try playing this with the right hand on the small tom.

R L R R L R R L R

REFERENCE   **"Theme For Penny"** 7th and 8th bar of bridge
during trumpet solo

album: *One for All*
A&M Records 75021 5329 4

Ex. 3k   Like in **3j**, you can play the right hand on the small tom-tom.

Play Time

R L R R L R

Ex. 3L   Variation   **3m**   (buzz unison hands)

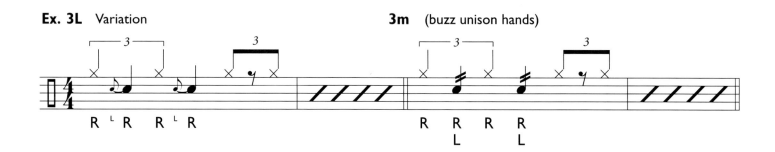

R L R R L R   R R R R
L L

"BLAKEY SHUFFLES"

Ex. 4a   Shuffle #1

[♩] = near edge of drum (closest to you)
V = deadstroke center of drum
(Firmly dig the stick into the drumhead — don't allow the stick to rebound or buzz.)

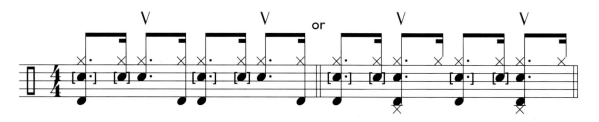

REFERENCE   **"Moanin'"** title cut
Blue Note BST 84003

"Dat Dere"

album: *The Big Beat*
Blue Note BST 84029 also

CD: *The History of Art Blakey and the Jazz Messengers*
Blue Note CDP 7 97190 2

Ex. 4b   Shuffle #2

REFERENCE **"Blues March"**
album: *Moanin'*
Blue Note BST 84003

Ex. 4c   Shuffle bossa

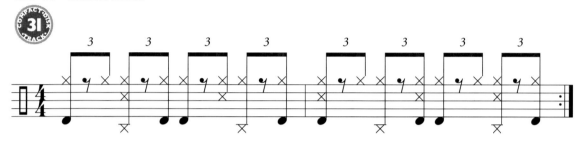

REFERENCE **"Pensativa"**
album: *Free for All*
Blue Note BN 84170

"BLAKEY MAMBOS"

Ex. 5a   Jazz mambo — even eighths

Art's Jazz Messages

The great drummer Kenny Clarke would often come to see the band when we played in Europe (he lived in Paris). One time the Big Band played in Torino, Italy, in the middle of a big soccer stadium. Kenny was playing in the festival the next night, so Art asked him if he wanted to play with the band during our show. I was stunned to find myself playing in a Big Band with three drummers — myself, Art Blakey and Kenny Clarke! I was even more stunned when I noticed Max Roach and the members of his percussion group M-Boom walking across the field toward the stage. Incidentally, Roy Haynes was there too, having just played the night before.

Another time when I was road manager for the Jazz Messengers I was backstage with Kenny Clarke at the New Morning Club in Paris. I had been road managing for sometime and I told Kenny I was frustrated because I hadn't been playing. Kenny said, "Yeah, you need to play with other people because that's where you get your ideas from."

That same evening Art gave me one of his two snare drums and told me to ask Kenny to tune it for him.

— *John Ramsay*

The next four examples are from the tune "A Night in Tunisia" on the album *A Night at Birdland* (Blue Note BN 1522 vol. 1; also heard on "Avilla Tequila", from the album *Jazz Messengers at the Café Bohemia*, vol. 2. (Blue Note BST 84090). The eighth notes can be slightly swung.

Ex. 5b

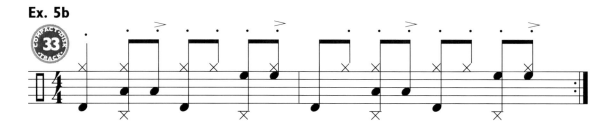

Ex. 5c

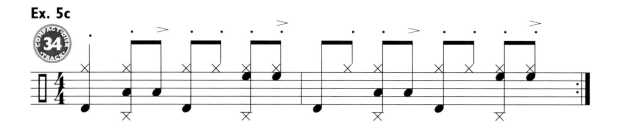

Ex. 5d

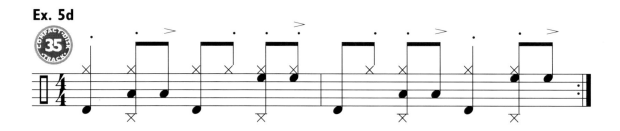

Ex. 5e

REFERENCE (5e only)   **"A Night in Tunisia"** bridge of the last melody chorus, bars 3-6

album: *A Night at Birdland*
Blue Note BN1522 vol. 1

Ex. 5f. This example has a $\frac{6}{8}$ Afro-Cuban feeling.

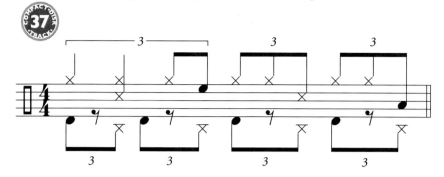

REFERENCE **"The Sortie"** B sections of the entire tune
album: *Indestructible*
Blue Note 8419

INSTRUMENTAL SOLO RESOLUTION

Art had a way of resolving or climaxing at the end of instrumental solos by playing into the next chorus and resolving after the end of the actual chorus. Here is a transcription of a video tape I have of Art playing with Johnny Griffin, Lockjaw Davis, and Illinois Jacquet. This happens at the end of Johnny Griffin's solo. The tune is "Take the A Train." The video is from a private collection and is not commercially available.

Ex. 6a

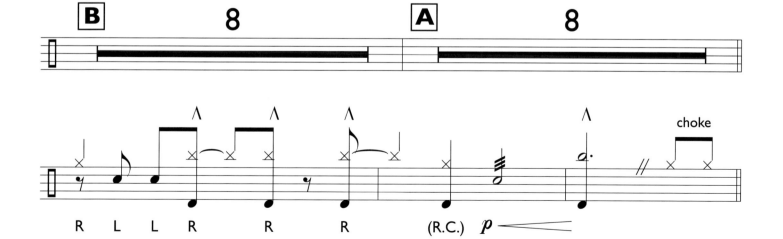

The next three examples are variations on how Art would extend the resolution of the soloists' blowing, into the beginning of the next chorus/soloist. All three are taken from the video *Jazz at the Smithsonian*. Example **6b** occurs in the tune "New York" at the end of Branford Marsalis's alto solo into the beginning of his brother Wynton's trumpet solo. Art uses two crash cymbals on his left.

Ex. 6b

• = struck with tip of stick

– = crash with shank of stick

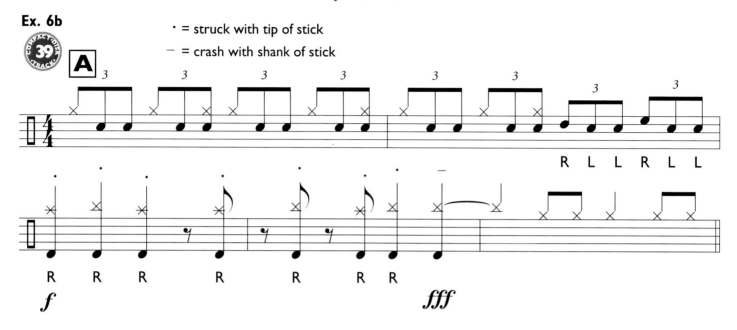

Ex. 6c In this example, Art starts figure **3b** (from Solo Licks) in the 8th bar of the last A section of the trumpet solo, into the 1st bar of the tenor solo first chorus.

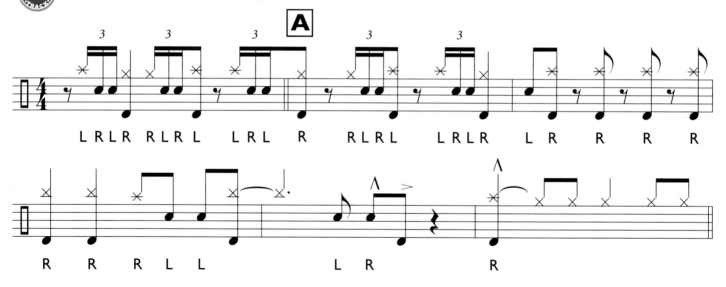

Ex. 6d

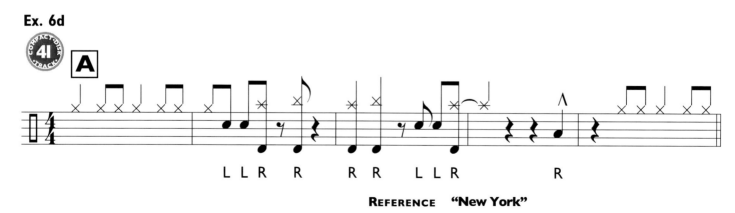

REFERENCE *"New York"*

Video: *Jazz at The Smithsonian*
1982 Sony Video LP

Examples **6e** and **6f** are very unusual beats. Art is the only drummer I've ever heard play them. Besides using them on "The Core" and "Fuller Love," in the early 1980's Art would also play this beat on the tune "Free for All." The difference between the above two examples is the hi-hat part. Art would most often play the hi-hat as shown on "Fuller Love," on beats 2 and 4.

Ex. 6e   "The Core" even eighths

ensemble
figures:

REFERENCE   **"The Core"** A sections of the tune

album: *Free for All*
Blue Note BN 84170

Ex. 6f   "Fuller Love" even eighths

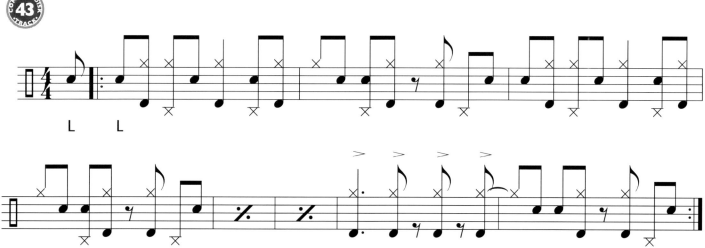

REFERENCE   **"Fuller Love"** A sections of the tune

album: *Keystone 3*
Concord Records CJ 196

Art had an interesting way of playing certain ensemble figures. While playing the figures with cymbals and bass drum, he would fill in notes on the snare drum (usually lightly ghosting the snare drum notes). The cymbals are crashed. This created a lot of intensity and excitement and, because of the alternating sticking on the cymbals, was visually exciting as well. Examples of this technique are shown in example **6g** and **6h**.

Ex. 6g

Ex. 6h

REFERENCE **"Fuller Love"** the bridge of the tune and the vamp at the end of the tune

album: *Album of the Year*
Timeless Records SJP 155

video: *The Jazz Life*
Myriad Media 1982

PLAYING ENSEMBLE FIGURES WITH UNISON FEET

Art would sometimes comp or play rhythmic figures with his feet playing in unison. The hi-hat could be played closed for short sounds or splashed for long sounds. The following example (**7a**) is from a 1982 recording.

Ex. 7a Shuffle

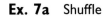

V = dead stroke

REFERENCE   **"One by One"** throughout the entire tune
Note: Art did not play this tune this way
on the original recording.

album: *Oh By the Way*
Timeless Records SJP 165

FLOATING THE TIME

In the following example Art creates a momentary feeling of half-time. He would refer to this particular device as "floating the time." Notice (on the recording) how quickly Branford Marsalis picks up on this rhythm. The eighth notes have a triplet feel.

Ex. 7b

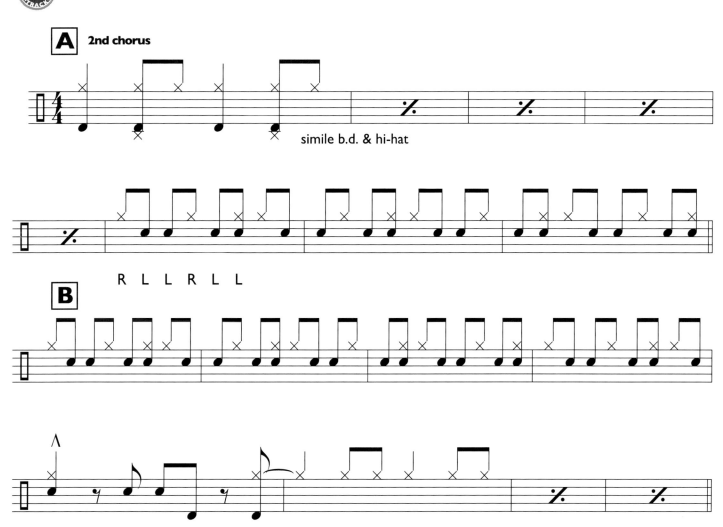

REFERENCE   **"In Walked Bud"** 2nd A section of the
2nd alto chorus

album: *Keystone 3*
Concord Records CJ 196

Ex. 7c With this example Art and pianist Sam Dockery play quarter note triplets within ⁴⁄₄ creating a momentary feeling of ³⁄₄.

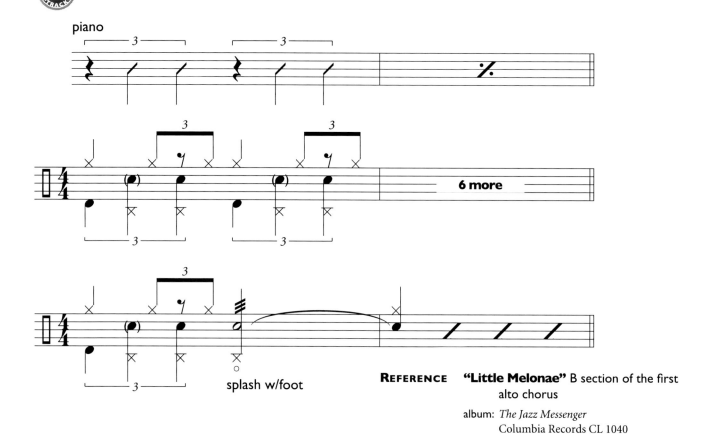

splash w/foot

REFERENCE   **"Little Melonae"** B section of the first alto chorus

album: *The Jazz Messenger*
Columbia Records CL 1040

Ex. 7d

Art's Jazz Messages

Once I asked Art if he was ever bothered by sore muscles and he said, "Sure! but you can't think about that."

Art always told his audience that "music was meant to wash away the dust of everyday life."

When we were in the studio outside Amsterdam making the record *Album of the Year*, after doing several takes of a tune I asked Art if he wanted to hear a playback. He replied, "What do I have to hear it for? I just played it."

Art once told me while I was playing a ballad, "You know you've got to play this (the hi-hat) softer too."

As road manager I frequently had to deal with people who wanted to be added to the guest list. Art had a standard line to deal with this; he would say, "If your friends won't pay to see you, who will?"

When I was eager to stop road managing Art would remind me that he had been Chick Webb's valet.

— *John Ramsay*

Art Blakey; Horace Silver Trio session, WOR studios, New York, Nov. 23, 1953

REFERENCE   CD: *Thelonius Monk: The Genius of Modern Music*, vol.1
CDP 7 81510 2

HUMPH

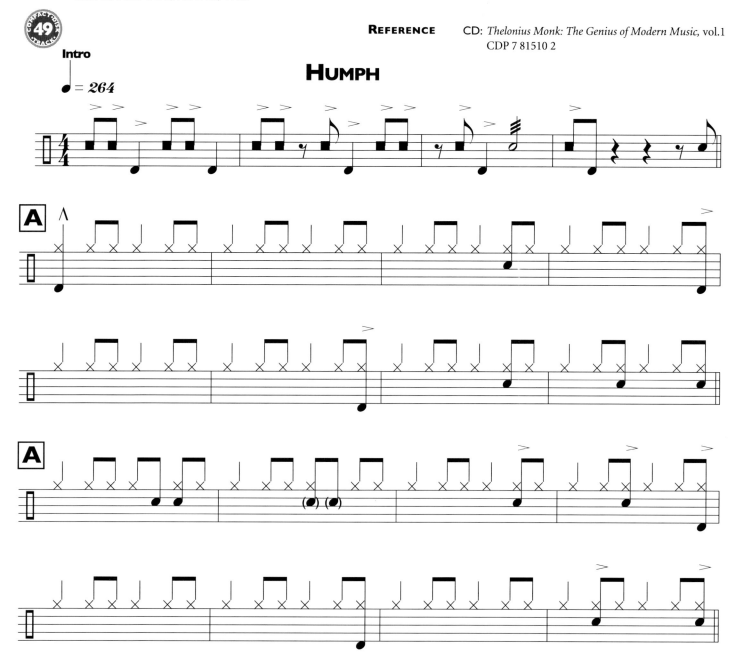

The interplay between Art and Monk in this example is very interesting and perhaps shows one reason why Blakey was Monk's favorite drummer.

REFERENCE **"Honeysuckle Rose"** (excerpt) call and response with Monk; 2nd A and bridge of 2nd piano solo chorus (after bass solo)

album: *The Riverside Trios*
Milestone Records M47052, originally

The Unique Thelonious Monk
Riverside Records 209

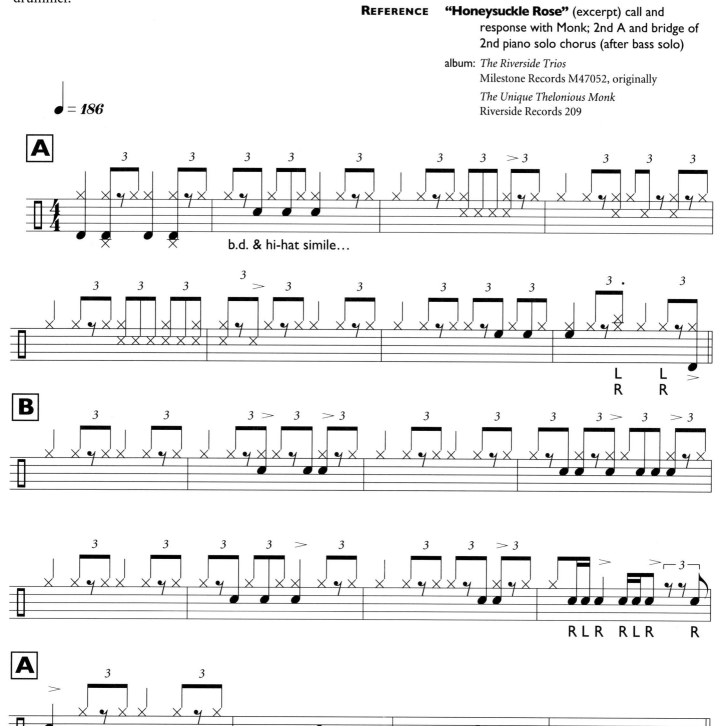

b.d. & hi-hat simile…

Ex. 1　The form is ABAC.
Quasi Latin feel

REFERENCE　"This I Dig of You"
album: *Soul Station* by Hank Mobley
Blue Note BAJ 84031

Head　　Play accents on the bell of the cymbal.

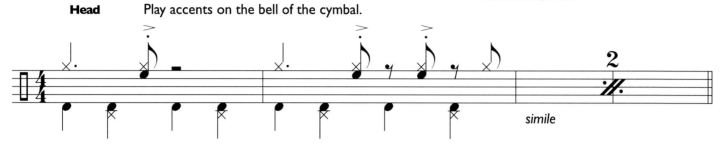

simile

Ex. 2　Behind piano solo

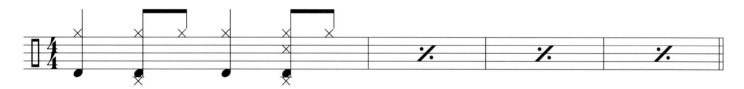

Ex. 3　C section of the 1st tenor chorus

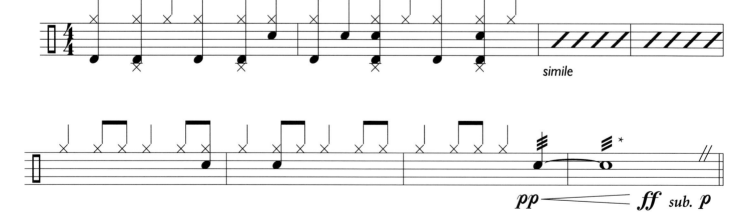

simile

pp —————— *ff* sub. *p*

* Art's famous press roll — here he builds in one
bar and the roll ends abruptly without a cymbal crash on one. Try an eighth note triplet
pulse for this roll.

Ex. 4   3rd tenor chorus

left cymbal bell

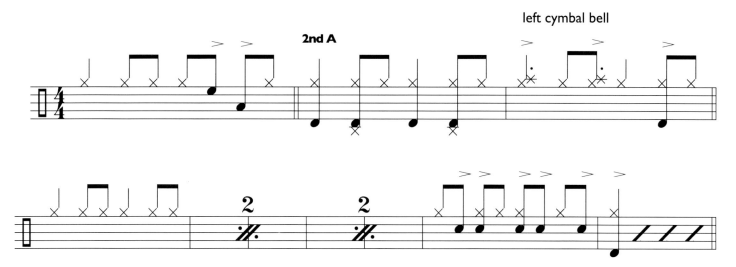

In the example below, Art keeps time with the right hand while crashing with the left hand on the crash cymbal, with the bass drum punctuating each cymbal crash. Another example of this technique can be heard on the melody chorus of "It's Only a Paper Moon" from *Art Blakey Live at the Renaissance Club.*

Ex. 5   5th tenor chorus. This is another example of how Art would imply ¾ in a ⁴⁄₄ tempo.

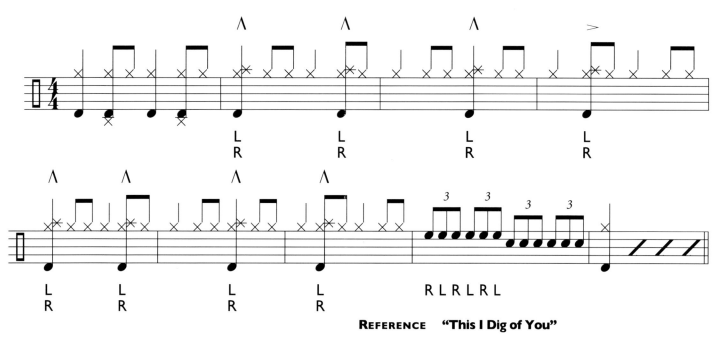

REFERENCE   *"This I Dig of You"*

album: *Soul Station* by Hank Mobley
Blue Note BAJ 84031

"Sportin' Crowd" ("Tenor Madness")
intro

♩ = *260*

On this recording it seems like the time gets turned around and the horns sound as if they come in backwards. Dig measures 5 and 6. Can you play them at ♩ = 260?

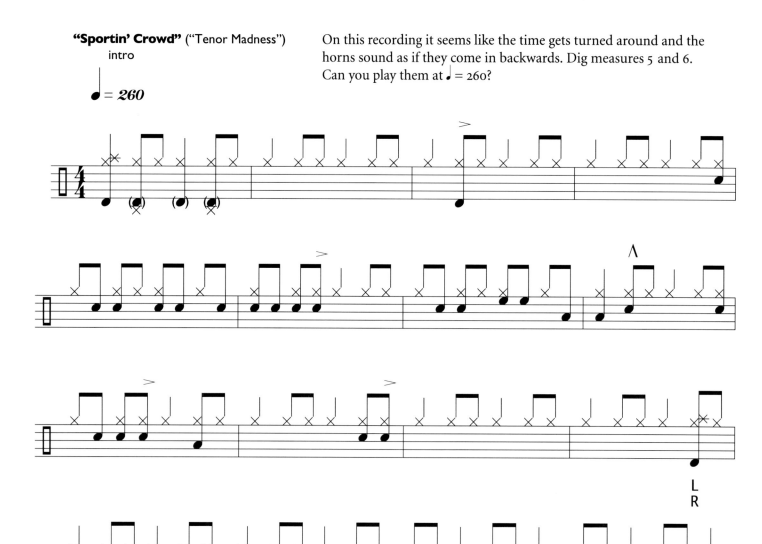

REFERENCE   **"Sportin' Crowd"** intro*

album: *The Jazz Messengers at the Cafe Bohemia* vol. 2
Blue Note BN 1508

* I believe the tune is actually Sonny Rollins's "Tenor Madness" and was mistitled on the album label.

Art's Jazz Messages

Many drummers have asked me if Art could read music. I always tell them the following story to illustrate how Art felt about reading music.

When I first joined the Big Band our debut was at The Bottom Line in New York City. I had written my own drum charts (there were none) to help me learn the tunes. During the first set after playing a few tunes, Art went to the microphone to introduce the band members and announce the names of the tunes. He then called a tune that we hadn't really rehearsed ("Jodi" by Walter Davis, Jr.). As he walked back to the drums he went behind me and told me to start the tune with a drum solo. I protested, saying that I didn't really know that tune. He said, "Just play!" I quickly pulled up my chart to "Jodi" that I had on a chair next to the drums and began my drum solo. After I played for a while Art gave me a nod and took over with his drum solo introduction. As he played his patented band lead in, I looked down at my drum charts and discovered that he had turned them all over. During the break Art chided me in the dressing room saying (to the rest of the band) "Fellas, you just gotta play! John's not playing, he's out there reading."

— ***John Ramsay***

TIMEKEEPING TRANSCRIPTION ¾ SWING

This is an example of the way Art kept time in ¾. The bass drum and the hi-hat are playing a strict ostinato in ¾ while the right hand plays the 4/4 jazz ride cymbal pattern over this. The effect is of a smooth and flowing jazz waltz.

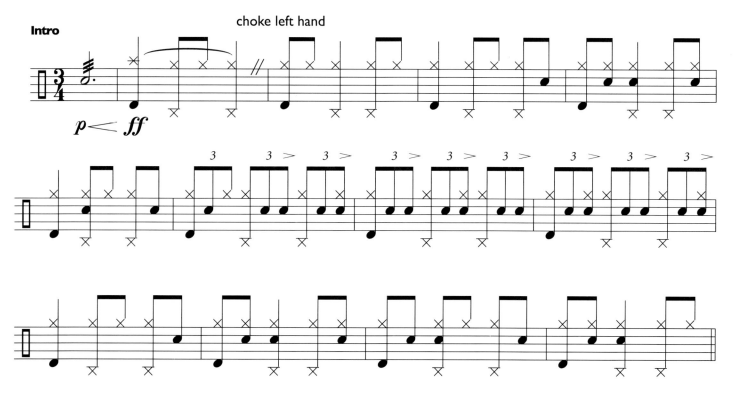

REFERENCE   **"Up Jumped Spring"** drum introduction
CD: *The History of Art Blakey and the Jazz Messengers*
Blue Note CDP 7 97190 2

UPTEMPO TIMEKEEPING (Blackbean Studio Audition)

The following examples were transcribed from my audition for the Jazz Messengers Big Band in New York City in 1980. We played the tune "E.T.A." at a very fast tempo and I experienced a great deal of difficulty keeping up. When the tune was over, Art very passionately gave me the following lecture:

"You got to hear with your eyes and see with your ears. What I don't hear is not true. Listen to what I'm doin'."

(plays the following example:)

simile b.d. and hi-hat …

Art would play a tempo like this by throwing his hand down from the wrist on the ride cymbal on beats 2 and 4, letting the other notes of the ride pattern bounce or rebound. I've indicated those notes with parentheses.

"It sounds fast. It's not that fast! It's just an intensity. Once you learn most problems with most drummers is they can't swing. The intensity, because you play soft, that don't mean … [unintelligible on tape] … That ain't got nothin' to do with it! All you got to do is …"

(plays the next example)

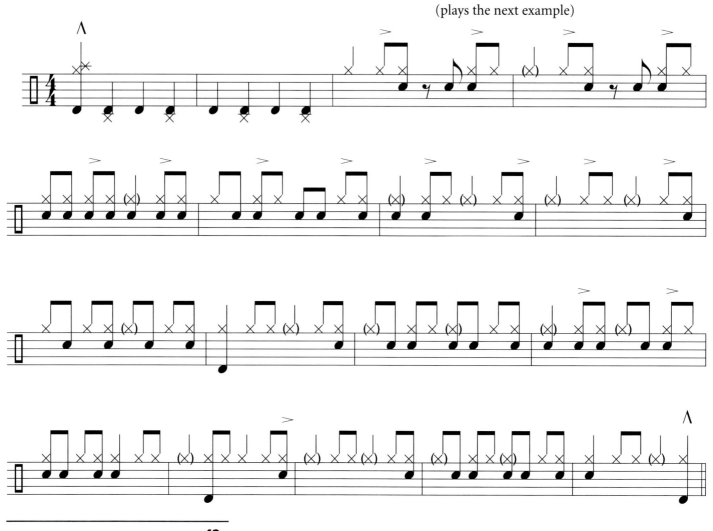

"The bass drum is goin' and the sock cymbal is goin'. But one thing — don't let your left hand know what your right hand is doin'. You got two hands and two feet and you ain't supposed to concentrate on no one thing. If you concentrate on your sock cymbal too much it makes the beat heavy and locks the musicians in. They can't solo and it makes it so heavy and the tempo drops. And they're out there fightin'. It's like throwing the soloist out in ice water with no boots. And you're supposed to be back there settin' a fire. That's the biggest problem! I can't understand it. And, it's mostly among black drummers. And it should never be! The first thing they should do is know how to swing. Forget all the technique! I'm not interested in the technique! 'Cause all the drummers sound like they all come off a conveyor belt. It's important, playing and identifying your-self. That's important, John, most important. Who's playing the drum? This is an instrument. It's not a melody instrument, but you s'posed to say, put on a record, it's Max Roach! That's Art Blakey! That's Elvin Jones! How you think it got that way? Cats have a certain thing that they do, that they never drop that beat. It's an intensity. They know if they play it with brushes, it still has that intensity. If you play it with sticks, it has that intensity. If you just play, say …

(plays the following)

That's s'posed to be happenin' all the time. Once you lose that [plays the above sloppily] that's what's goin' to happen to you. All you got to do is relax and I can't tell you how to do that. It's so difficult. It's hard. All you got to do is relax.

Don't do that, whenever you do it if you get into it, I'll tell you 'lay out — I'll take it.' Then you come back in. Don't be afraid to stop, because it'll mess up the whole band."

Art's Jazz Messages

Quotes from Art Blakey: From the video, Jazzmakers, *a Chevron School Broadcast Production.*

I do things my way. I may grab a stick backwards or a heavy stick in the left hand or a light one on the right hand or a heavy one on the right, it doesn't make any difference to me. What I want is to accomplish what I'm after and what's runnin' through my mind. You just play! You know what I mean? You're sup-posed to be playin' in such a way, in such a spiritual way, you take the whole audience and put them right inside your drum.

— **Art Blakey**

Another example of Art's uptempo comping

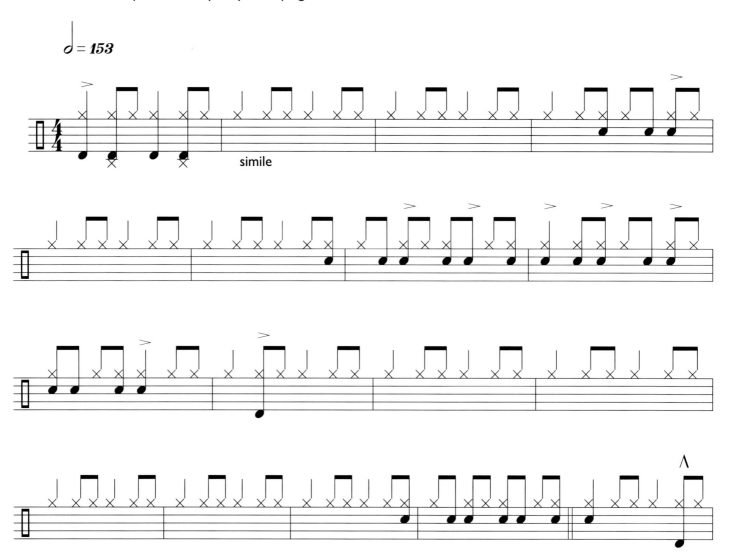

$\circ$ = *153*

simile

REFERENCE   **"Justice"** first 17 bars of the trumpet solo

CD: *The History of Art Blakey and the Jazz Messengers*
Blue Note CDP 7 97190 2

Art's Jazz Messages

From the video, Jazzmakers, *a Chevron School Broadcast Production.*

This is a team, this is a band. We have no stars. The star is the whole band. We all work together. We all need each other.

Music is just a wonderful thing and it's good medicine, it's really good medicine. I don' care how sick I am, I can have a temperature of 105 or 106, I don't care. I get to my drums, get to the bandstand and BASH! after the first note, and I never know how I feel that day until I hit the first note, because the

adrenaline comes up and you're just playing and whatever sickness it was, is gone.

You gotta create your own identity. That's the most important thing on any instrument. This is your job to go up there and make people feel good. This is the idea about jazz. This is the wonderful thing about it. This is what makes jazz the eighth wonder of the world. Because we don't know what we're gonna play. No music, (written) from the creator, to the artist, to you. Split second timing.

— *Art Blakey*

THREE BLIND MICE

REFERENCE   CD: *The History of Art Blakey and the Jazz Messengers*
Blue Note CDP 7 97190 2

Bend note with elbow by pushing it into snare drum head (with snares off)

tenor solo

simile …

trombone solo

trumpet solo

Bend note with elbow by pushing it into snare drum head
(with snares off)

straight eighths

Art used a four-piece set until the 1970s when he added a tom-tom, using two mounted toms (8x12 and 9x13). When I joined the big band in 1980 Pearl Drums provided us with two seven-piece kits (three mounted toms and two floor toms). Art used this type of set until he died.

Key

10" tom   12" tom   13" tom   14" tom   16" tom

Ex. 1a   Art's favorite solo lick. Art played this lick during virtually all of his solos.

R L R L R   R   L R L R

REFERENCE   **"Justice"** 1st and 6th bar of the drum solo

CD: *The History of Art Blakey and the Jazz Messengers*
Blue Note CDP 7 97190 2

Ex. 1b   Longer, with more drums

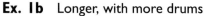
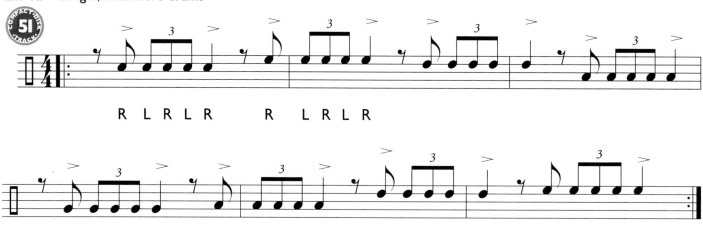

R L R L R   R   L R L R

Ex. 1c Snares off

R L R L R   R   L R L R   R L R L   R

L R

REFERENCE   **"A Night in Tunisia"** (title cut) 9th bar of drum intro

album: *A Night in Tunisia*
Blue Note BN 84049

Ex. 1d ∧ = rim shot

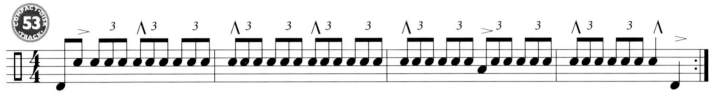

R L R L R L R

REFERENCE   **"Theme For Penny"** intro

album: *One for All*
A&M Records 75021 5329 4

Art's Jazz Messages

Sometimes Art would play quarter notes on the ride cymbal by playing his right hand in large circular (clockwise) motions, sideswiping the cymbal at the bottom part of the circle. You can hear him doing this on the tune "Theme for Penny" on the A&M record *One for All*.

One time in Japan the Jazz Messengers were playing with two drummers, Art and George Kawaguchi. During the break tune Art went to the microphone to talk and I took his seat at the drums to play. As the intensity built (after Art spoke) I began to play harder, actually hitting harder. Art came up behind me and said "No, no! If you want to build the intensity do it this way." He then proceeded to play the cymbal by playing first with the tip of the stick on the outermost part of the cymbal and then playing into it more with the shank of the stick. This created a kind of underlying roar that did indeed build the intensity, but with the least amount of effort.

When Art came to Boston to receive an honorary doctorate from Berklee College of Music, he asked Billy Pierce and myself what was happening in town that evening. When we told him there was a jam session at the 1369 Jazz Club he wanted to go. While we were sitting around in the basement office chatting with the club owners I went upstairs to the bar; as I passed the bandstand the musicians asked me if I wanted to sit in and play. I was unaware that while I was playing, below me in the office Art said to Billy Pierce, "Who's that playing drums up there? It sounds like John." When I returned to the office Art leaned over to me and said, "John, when you play, you don't have to prove nothin', all you have to do is swing."

— **John Ramsay**

Art got me two times like that [like the story about the 1369 Jazz Club]. The first time was when I first joined the band; we were down at Fat Tuesday's. Actually, we were auditioning for the band and Wynton was still there. Art told me, he said, "Man, now you're a Jazz Messenger. Don't worry about Freddie Hubbard, Woody Shaw, or none of them cats — I want you to be you! I want you to be yourself." And, like that really . . .ed me up because I never put myself on the level — I still don't — of those cats, but I think the thing he was saying was, you know, they're human beings just like everybody else, and I just have to work on my strength. And, develop my weaknesses as well.

— **Terence Blanchard**
TRUMPET; February 1982–March 1985

Ex. 1e

R L R L R   R L R L R

Ex. 1f   Intro or band lead-in   ■ = stick on stick

R L R L R   L R R

Ex. 1g   Variation of 1a

R L R L R

REFERENCE   **"Avilla Tequilla"** drum intro

   album: *Jazz Messengers at the Café Bohemia* vol. 2
         Blue Note 1508; also on

   CD: *The History of Art Blakey and the Jazz Messengers*
        Blue Note CDP 7 97190 2

Ex. 1h   1a. at fast tempos

even eighths

R L R L

REFERENCE   **"Buhaina's Delight"** title cut, during the
        drum solo

   album: *Buhaina's Delight*
        Blue Note BN 4104

Ex. 1i   More implied ⁴/₄. Play this with matched grip; use the butt of
       the stick in the left hand.

L R L R L R   L R L R L R

REFERENCE   **"Honeysuckle Rose"** 5th–8th bars of the
        drum solo

   album: *Thelonious Monk Riverside Sessions*
        Riverside Records 4004 2

Ex. 1j These examples remind me of rolling thunder. Art looks like he might have been playing these figures in the photo below.

snares off

R   L   R   L   R   L   R   L

Jymie Merritt, Lee Morgan and Art Blakey at the Jazz Gallery, July 1961

Ex. 1k At faster tempos

R   L   R   L   R   L   R   L

REFERENCE **"Those Who Sit and Wait"** 6th four-bar drum solo of trading fours

album: *The Witch Doctor*
Blue Note BST 84258

Ex. 1l

Ex. 1m at faster tempos

L   R   L   R   R   L   R   L   L   R   L   R   L   R   L   R

REFERENCE **"Sortie"** the 4th drum fill of ending vamp

album: *Indestructible*
Blue Note BN84193

LEAD-INS

Ex. 2a Art's famous band lead-in: Art ended virtually all of his drum solos this way.

R   L   R   L   R L R L R L R   R   L R L R   R   L R L R

REFERENCE **"Free for All"** title cut, end of drum solo

album: *Free for All*
Blue Note (8) 4170

Ex. 2b   Variation of **2a**

R   L R   L   R L R L R R   L R   R

Ex. 2c

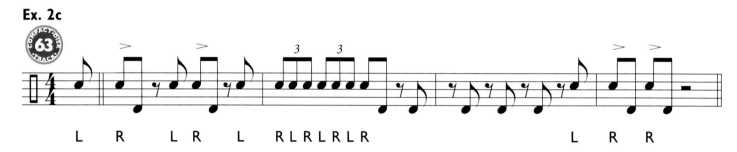

L   R   L R   L   R L R L R L R   L   R   R

REFERENCE   **"Minor Thesis"** end of drum solo

album: *Art Blakey and the Jazz Messengers Big Band*
Timeless Records SJP 150

I first heard Art play this in the late 1980's, which showed
me that he was still trying to discover new things.

Ex. 2d   **Ex. 2e**   **Ex. 2f**   **Ex. 2g**

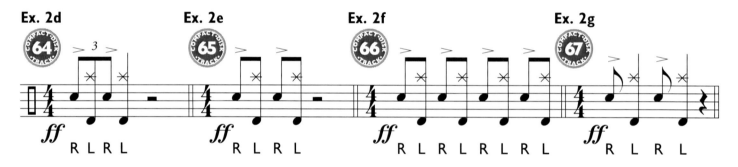

ff R L R L   *ff* R L R L   *ff* R L R L R L R L   *ff* R L R L

REFERENCE   **"Here We Go"**

album: *One for All*
A&M Records 75021 5329 4 (1990)

Ex. 2h   A single-stroke roll between the right hand and right foot.
Try moving the right hand around the drums randomly.

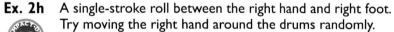

R   R   R   R   R   R   R   R

REFERENCE   **"Free for All"** 10th & 11th bars of the
2nd A of the head

CD: *The History of Art Blakey and the Jazz Messengers*
Blue Note CDP 7 97190 2

Ex. 3a Art would always grab the listener's attention when he played this. It would usually happen between the soloists' phrases. Play this very aggressively.

R L R L R L   R L R L R L

REFERENCE "A Night in Tunisia" 8th bar of the 1st A section of 2nd alto chorus

album: *A Night at Birdland* Blue Note 1522 vol. 1

The following are variations of a four-stroke ruff. Art would break them up between cymbals and snare drum.

Ex. 3b

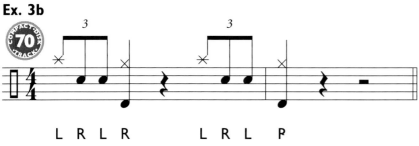

L R L R   L R L P

Ex. 3c

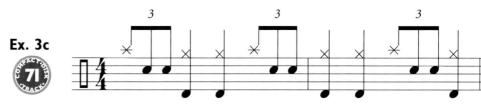

L R L R   R   L R L   R   R   L R L R

Ex. 3d

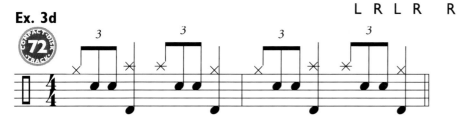

R L R L   L R L R   R L R L   L R L R

Ex. 3e

L R L R   L R L R   L R L   R

Ex. 3f Double strokes

R R L L R   R R L L R

REFERENCE (3f only) "Little Melonae" 2nd A section of 3rd alto chorus, 8th bar

album: *The Jazz Messenger* Columbia Records CL 1040

Examples **3g** and **3h** are usually played as part of a longer phrase. I have
written them here individually so that they may be learned more easily.
A version of the longer phrase is seen in example **3i**.

Ex. 3g   **Ex. 3h**

REFERENCE   **"Arabia"** the end of the drum solo

CD: *The History of Art Blakey and the Jazz Messengers*
Blue Note CDP 7 97190 2

Ex. 3i

REFERENCE   **"Minor Thesis"** 5th bar of the extended drum
solo after the shout chorus

album: *Art Blakey and the Jazz Messengers Big Band*
Timeless Records SJP150

Ex. 4a "Afro Tom-Toms" (hi-hat & B.D. throughout)

I call these Afro-Toms because they remind me of something African sounding. Art had a lot of variations. Here's the most basic one, for one drum. Lightly ghost the left hand.

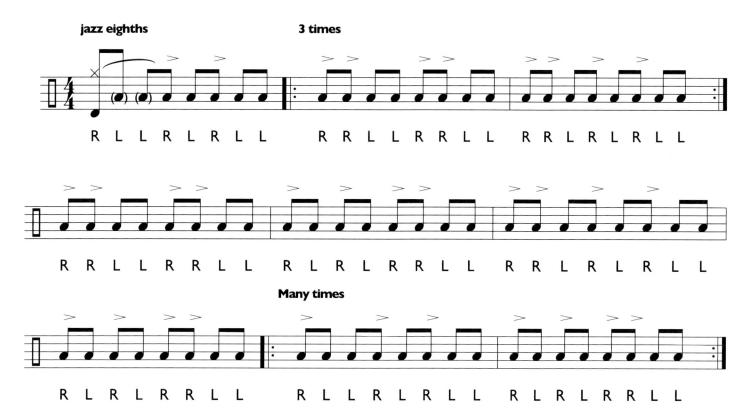

REFERENCE   **"Arabia"** opening bars of drum solo

CD: *The History of Art Blakey and the Jazz Messengers*
Blue Note CDP 7 97190 2

Other variations I've seen Art play:

Variation of **4a**, with Afro-toms, snares off

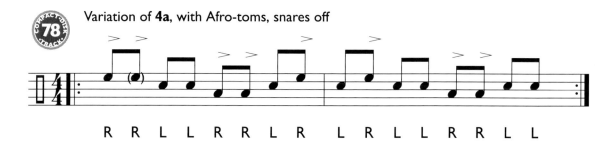

REFERENCE   **"A Night in Tunisia"** 1st four bars of drum solo

album: *A Night at Birdland*
Blue Note 1522 vol. 1

Art's Jazz Messages

Although the musical director would call the tunes in the set, sometimes Art would change it.

— *Billy Pierce*

TENOR SAXOPHONE; December 1979–September 1982

Ex. 4b Two floor toms: 14" & 16"

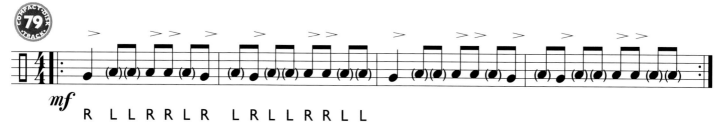

mf
R L L R R L R L R L L R R L L

Ex. 4c Played as part of CD track 79

f *sfz*

R L R L R L L R L L R R L R L R L L R R L L

REFERENCE **"Gypsy Folktales"**
video: *The Jazz Life*
Myriad Media 1982

MORE AFRO-TOMS

Ex. 4d

R R L L R R L L

Ex. 4e

R R L L R R L L R R L L

REFERENCE **"Gypsy Folktales"** drum solo
video: *The Jazz Life*
Myriad Media 1982

December 25, 1992, anecdotes from pianist Donald Brown.

Art once told me: "Look, I like the way you comp and I like the way you play but just relax, 'cause you're up here with me and they're out there and you don't have a thing to prove. The only thing you owe me is to swing me, and to swing me into the ground."

A lot of times Bu (short for Buhaina, Art's Muslim name) could tell I was nervous about playing solo piano and he would always tell me: "Look, don't make a big deal out of it. It should be just like at home playin' in your living room." Whenever he put it that way it helped me relax; you're not worried about how you'd mess up or anything.

— **Donald Brown**
Piano; July 1981–July 1982
September 1986–April 1987

Ex. 4f

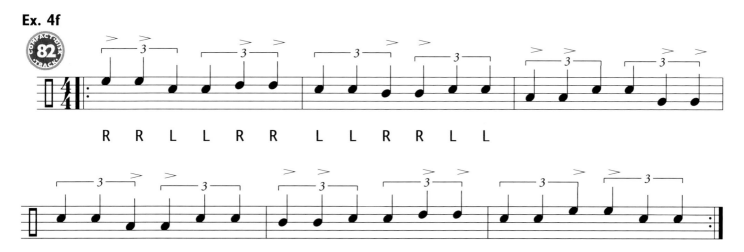

REFERENCE   **"Gypsy Folktales"** drum solo introduction
     video: *The Jazz Life*
           Myriad Media 1982

AFRO-CUBAN FEEL

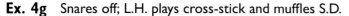

Ex. 4g   Snares off; L.H. plays cross-stick and muffles S.D.

REFERENCE   **"Gypsy Folktales"** drum solo intro
     video: *The Jazz Life*
           Myriad Media 1982
     album: *A Night in Tunisia* title cut (during drum solo)
           Blue Note 84049

Ex. 4h   Variation of ex. 4g

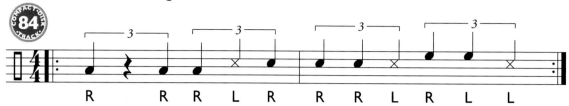

REFERENCE   **"A Night in Tunisia"** 5th bar of 2nd A section
during 3rd drum solo chorus

album: *A Night in Tunisia*
Blue Note 84049

Ex. 5a

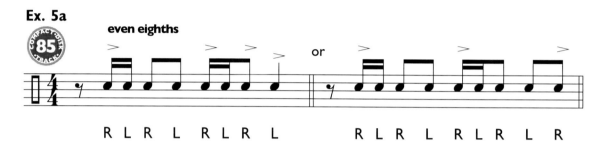

REFERENCE   **"Free for All"** last bar of the first A section
on the head

CD: *The History of Art Blakey and the Jazz Messengers*
Blue Note CDP 7 97190 2

Ex. 5b

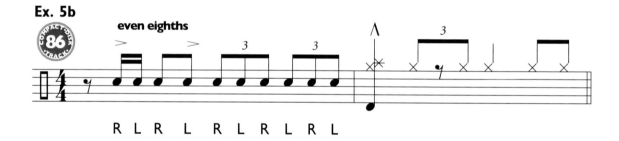

Ex. 5c

REFERENCE   **"Arabia"** beginning in the 2nd bar of the 2nd A
section of 2nd drum solo chorus

CD: *The History of Art Blakey and the Jazz Messengers*
Blue Note CDP 7 97190 2

Ex. 5d Unison hands & feet; even eighths

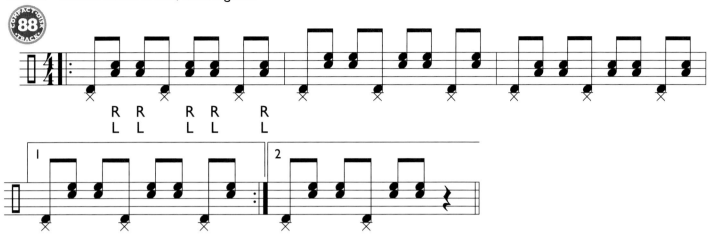

REFERENCE **"Split Kick"** bar 29 of drum solo
album: *A Night at Birdland* vol. 1
Blue Note BLP1521

Ex. 5e

♩ = *150*

ff R L R L R L

or

R L R L R L

REFERENCE **"Avilla Tequilla"** drum solo after the piano solo
CD: *The History of Art Blakey and the Jazz Messengers*
Blue Note CDP 7 97190 2

Art's Jazz Messages

Quotes from Art Blakey from the video Jazzmakers, *a Chevron School Broadcast Production:*

Music, it's good, it's good to have it in the house; just like havin' flowers in the house, it's beautiful. We should listen to all kinds of music — everything. Mostly what we do is done to some kind of music. If a child is born they play music. If you die, they play music. They play when you march off to war. Music is a very important thing. Music to wake up by, music to sleep by, music to dance by, all kinds of music.

Every night I surprise myself. Sure that's the way you have fun and get surprised. You gotta keep on innovating — find new things. And you can make a mistake and turn around and make the same mistake and make something out of it. And then out of it comes something new and it keeps movin' on.

This is real democracy in action. Each one of us puttin' in his part and it comes out to be one big beautiful arrangement.

— *Art Blakey*

Ex. 5f With this figure Art keeps the grace notes of the flams on the snare drum, with the right hand moving around the toms.

even eighths

Or sometimes ended this way:

REFERENCE   **"Cheryl"** 2nd fours of drum "fours"

album: *Album of the Year*
Timeless Records SJP 155

Ex. 6a With this lick Art would hold the left stick very loosely while striking it with the right stick. The left stick would rebound creating a ³⁄₈ rhythm. In this example the right hand plays a dotted quarter note rhythm. Try other rhythms; try starting the figure off the beat.

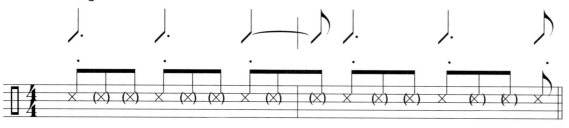

REFERENCE   **"Are You Real?"** 3rd fours on trading "fours"

album: *Moanin'*
Blue Note 4003

Art's Jazz Messages

I remember one time Art got us with Billy Pierce in the band. You know, because we had been playing those same backgrounds night after night after night. Boy, he got tired of hearin' that shit. Boy, he went off on us! "Goddammit mother . . . .ers, use your imagination! Shit, you play that same shit over and over again. Goddammit, that's why I hired you. You're Jazz Messengers now; you ain't gotta worry about that . . . .in' shit out there. Use your . . . .in' imagination."

And then another time he caught me; I had been playing like Miles Davis; bro', you were still with us. You remember when I was playing "My Funny Valentine," and I used to play with the mute all the time? Man, he pulled me aside, he said "Goddammit Terence, you ain't no mother. . . .in' Miles Davis. I told him about that shit. You gotta play the . . . .in' melody, mother. . . .er. You gotta play the melody; don't nobody know what the . . . . you' playin'."

— *Terence Blanchard*

Ex. 6b Art employed the following during solos by placing the right stick under the left stick (which is held firmly into the drum-head) and moving the right stick up and down.

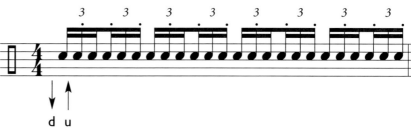

REFERENCE   **"Are You Real"** 3rd fours on trading "fours"

album: *Moanin'*
Blue Note 4003; also

"The Theme" during drum solo

album: *Cafe Bohemia* vol. 1
Blue Note 1507

Art at Lee Morgan's "Leeway" session, Englewood Cliffs, NJ, August 28, 1960

Ex. 6c

REFERENCE   **"The Opener"** drum solo

album: *Meet You at the Jazz Corners of the World* vol. 1
Blue Note BN 84054

BONUS SOLOS: TWO OF ART'S FAVORITES

Ex. 6d This is interesting because of the way the sticking sets up the accent scheme in bars 4, 8 and 12. Play the right strokes softly. Art would sometimes play this figure with the left hand crossing over the right to play the accented notes on the tom-toms.

*see figure **6a**

Ex. 6e   Another one of Art's favorites

even eighths

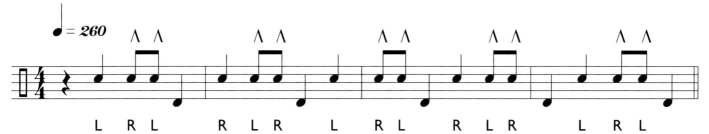

L   R   L   R   L   R   L   L   R   L   R   L   R   L   R   L

R   L   R   L   R   L   R   L

Art Blakey, Jymie Merritt, and Lee Morgan at the Jazz Gallery, 1961

Art's Jazz Messages

I remember one time when we played in Montreal and I was playing real close to the mike and Art told me he wanted to teach me how to play with a mike. He said, "What you do is when you start off your solo you get close to the mike and you play softly and then as you build in intensity back away from it a little more and by the third or fourth chorus you should be … [I forget how many inches he said —

I think it was two or three inches away from the mike]. Just so you could pick up the intensity." You know, he'd been listening to Fats (Navarro) and watching Sarah Vaughan. You know he said a whole lot of stuff; you just can't remember all of it. I mean some of it's so ingrained in you, it becomes second nature.

— *** Wallace Roney ***
Trumpet; May 1981–September 1986

4 SOLO TRANSCRIPTIONS

REFERENCE **"Split Feelins"**

album: *Soul Station* by Hank Mobley
Blue Note BAJ 84031

Trading "fours" with tenor

Bend note with elbow by pushing it into snare drum head (with snares off)

snares off

snares off

right stick under left stick
(see p. 71, fig. **6b**)

This is a classic Blakey solo. You will find many of his trademark ideas here. I think it's an example of a perfectly constructed drum solo. Notice the use of space.

REFERENCE   **"This I Dig of You"**

album: *Soul Station* by Hank Mobley
Blue Note BAJ 84031

Much of the tradition of jazz drumming comes from marching bands. I watched Art play this tune many times before I realized he was playing a four stroke roll (the pickups to bar 1, etc.).

REFERENCE   **"Blues March"**

album: *Art Blakey and the Jazz Messengers at Club St. Germain* vol. 2
RCA records 900.070

March

Sometimes Art would play solos that incorporated timekeeping. Here, he uses both classic Blakey timekeeping and solo ideas.

REFERENCE   "Honeysuckle Rose"

album: *Thelonious Monk the Riverside Trios*
Riverside Records 4004-2 or
Milestone Records M-47052

album: *Thelonious Monk the Riverside Trios*
Riverside Records 4004-2 or
Milestone Records M-47052

AABA form

Solo intro; hi-hat on 2 and 4 throughout

+ = Left crosses over right.

Art probably played this solo with matched grip, playing the left hand with the butt end of the stick. Play the drums forcefully. And of course listen to the original recording! The accent pattern sets up a 3/8 feeling.

REFERENCE   "What Know"

album: *Meet You at the Jazz Corner of the World* vol. 1
Blue Note 84054

REFERENCE   **"Nutty"**

album: *Monk with Sonny Rollins*
Prestige Records LP 7075

Hi-hat on 2 and 4 throughout

The term "head" is what jazz musicians call the
melody chorus of a tune to differentiate between the
improvised solo choruses and the original melody.

REFERENCE **"Kelo"**

album: *Miles Davis*
Blue Note BN 1501 vol. 1 1953

* An example of the way Art would play some ensemble figures with unison feet.

choke

trumpet break

Art's Jazz Messages

You know one thing you gotta put in there [the Blakey book] that a lot of people forget about Art. Art was here before Max [Roach] in an historical context. And another thing was Art was the first really polyrhythmic drummer. Art was really the first one to put triplets on the snare drum while riding. He was the first one to do that; before Elvin [Jones],

before Roy [Haynes]. You ask Elvin. Elvin told me, he said, "Anyone that plays anything modern comes from Art Blakey." But my man was Buhaina [Art Blakey], that's my man. He'd do anything for me and I'd do anything for him. Nobody, if you look in history from 1943, any of that, Klook [Kenny Clarke] didn't play those triplets on there.

— ***Wallace Roney***

With this tune and all the tunes in this section
be sure to check out the melodies on the
recordings to see why Art played what he did.

REFERENCE *"Cheryl"*

album: *Album of the Year*
Timeless Records SJP 155

Tenor solo

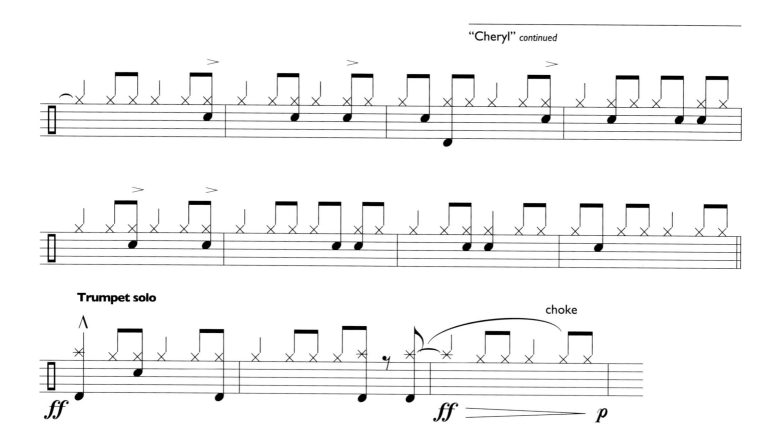

Trumpet solo

Benny Green and I shared a delightful conversation over lunch in Perugia, Italy, in July of 1993. When I told him about this book and its many transcriptions, he said "Oh yeah, I know some stuff you could never transcribe."

We both knew immediately that he was talking about "Free for All," particularly what occurs after the following transcription. It's some of the most inspired and explosive music you will ever hear — check it out!

REFERENCE **"Free for All"** head only

album: *Free for All*
  Blue Note 84170 or

CD: *The History of Art Blakey and the Jazz Messengers*
  Blue Note CDP 7 97190 2

Intro

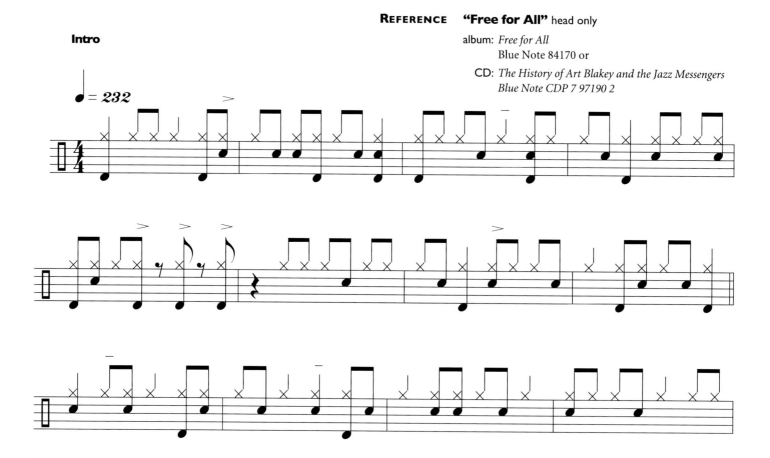

This is another example of how Art would keep
time with the right hand on the ride cymbal,
while playing ensemble figures in the left hand
with the crash cymbal and bass drum.

REFERENCE   "Ms. B.C."
video: The Jazz Life
Myriad Media

Art Blakey at Small's, October 1959

REFERENCE   **"Infra Ray"**

album: *The Jazz Messenger*
Columbia Records (cassette) CT 47118

During my time as Art's road manager (Fall 1980–Fall 1982) I kept a record of various band business in little pocket notebooks I always carried with me. During the band's performances, I would stand backstage ready to deal with sound monitor problems or other equipment troubles. Frequently, I would record in the notebooks things of interest to me that Art played on the drums. Consequently, interspersed throughout the notebooks with band draws (pay advances), hotel information, foreign currency, and other data, there were various drum notations. These ideas were really the seeds for this book, and appear here transcribed exactly as they appeared in my original notebooks.

SOME EXCERPTS FROM MY NOTEBOOKS...

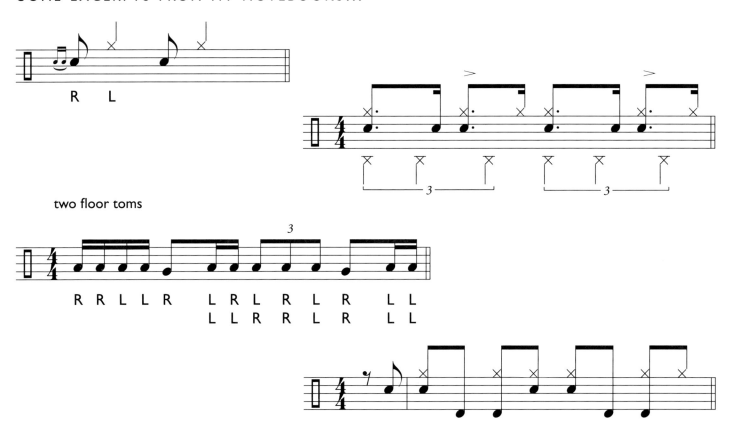

two floor toms

FROM MARCH 25, 1981
Paris/Dusseldorf

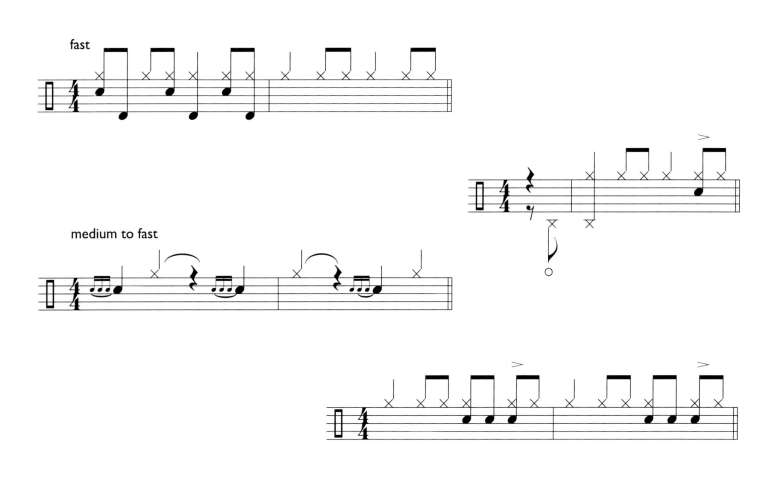

L R L R (L.H. rim click; R.H. stick on stick)

very fast

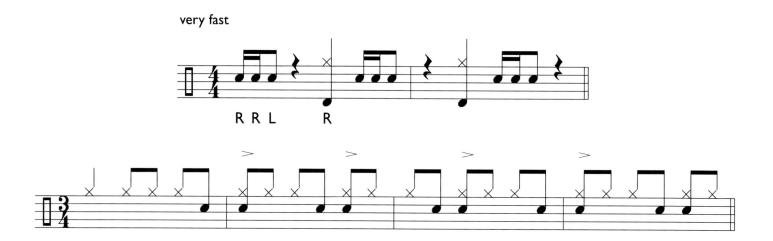

R R L   R

unison — cym. or tom-tom

At the ends of tunes, Art would sometimes play
elaborate cadenza-like endings. The following
is an example of one of those cadenzas.

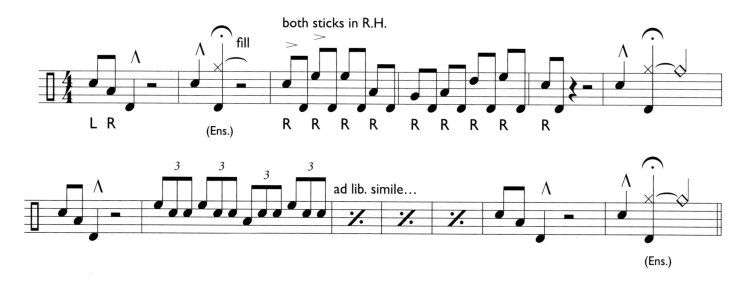

up tempo

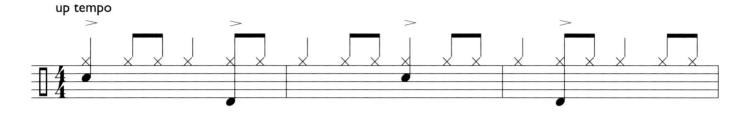

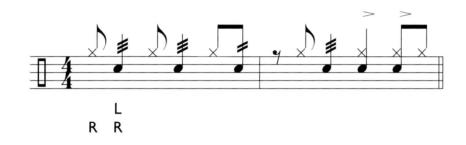

L
R   R

slow shuffle

rebound

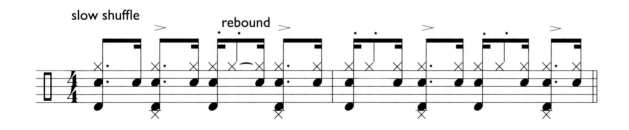

fast

The tune "E.T.A.," a Bobby Watson composition, played very fast.

R L R L R L R L

R L R L R L

ballad: double-time feel

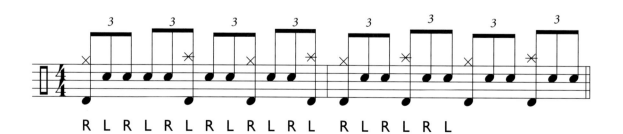

R L R L R L R L R L R L R L   R L R L R L

L R L R R L R L R R

One time when I was playing with the Big Band Art said, "You gotta relax, [when you play] I've got my way, you've gotta find your way."

Regarding solos: "Don't try to build your whole career in one solo."

— *John Ramsay*

Art told me, "On ballads take your time and tell a story. Play the melody."

— *Billy Pierce*

med. fast   Crash cymbals suspended time effect; fill in on S.D.

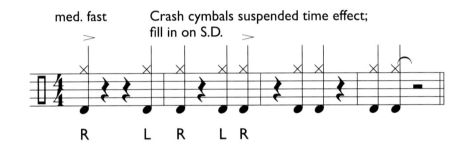

R   L   R   L   R

R L R L R   R L R L R

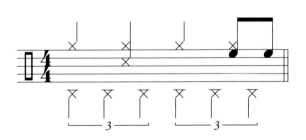

L   R

even eighths

Possible ghost L.H.   L.H.—mambo

"Witchhunt" tempo; L.H. (snare drum) plays busy double-time phrases.

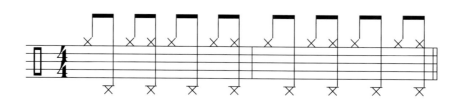

"Alamode" Play shuffle with double-time H.H.

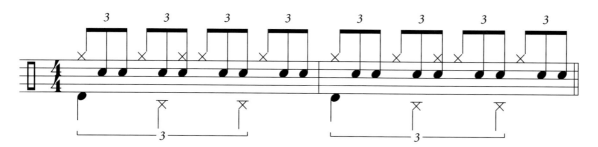

Throughout the course of writing this book the idea of Art's Jazz Messages that appear throughout the book was an evolving one (thanks to Bill Brinkley for the design concept). Originally, I remembered many things that Art had told me personally, and decided to query other Jazz Messengers about what he may have told them. What started with short meetings in night-club dressing rooms, hotel lobbies, and jazz festivals later evolved into more formal and lengthy interviews, in person and over the phone. What follows are those interviews, with, for the most part, very little editing.

BENNY GREEN

PIANO; April 1987–October 1989

Art said to me, "You have to figure out a way to get beyond Art Tatum." He said it to me on a few different occasions and whenever he would say it I would usually break into laughter because I figured he was teasin' me (because the piano can't be played better than Art Tatum played it). But I've thought about it a lot since and the way I like to interpret what he was saying and perhaps what he really meant, is you have to get beyond imitating any influence; anyone who's been a musical hero or an inspiration should serve as a means to spur you on to new heights of creativity and individuality (rather than just seeing what they did as a finality). So I believe that's what he really meant. Rather than say, play the piano faster than Art Tatum played it or more proficiently, I think he meant: get beyond just looking at someone else's contribution in awe and really get down to the heart of the matter, [which] in jazz is really developing your own voice as an individual.

There were a lot of important lessons that Art dropped on us at different times depending on what was called for. It's interesting how it's been several years since I played with the Messengers and yet musical situations will arise and something will occur to me that he said to me at some point and subconsciously I stored it way back in my memory bank and it invariably holds true and is very profound. There's one thing that I don't keep too far beneath the surface, that I try to keep in mind at all times that he directed to me personally.

That had to do with consistency as a performer and the responsibilities of the musician in terms of our role or our duty to uplift the spirits of listeners, of the audience who come to hear us. That means even though we're mortal human beings before we're musicians, when you step on the bandstand, the bandstand is sacred ground and you need to really shed certain self-centered aspects of your humanity. If there's something going on emotionally or psychologically or physically that has you fatigued or drained, you have to discard that and really strive to realize your higher purpose as a musician — to be an instrument for the music and be able to bring the listeners together spiritually with the power of the music. And that was really in keeping with what Art used to say about the music being from the creator to the artist direct to the audience — split second timing; and for myself he would talk about consistency. He would say one night you sound this way, another night you sound another way, and that's fine but just always make sure that nothing is on your mind or is going on in your life that would ever get in the way or block the flow of the music.

Another thing in keeping with that whole theme of consistency and delivery as a performer that he directed at me, was the fact that when people came to hear the Messengers, as Art put it — I'm sure a lot of drummers may disagree — but the way Art put it, he said they really came to hear the Messengers, not so much to hear himself, they came to hear the young cats that he had gotten together, to hear what they had to say. And he used to tell me "I've earned my respect and I've earned my reputation, yours has yet to be established so you have to go out there and prove yourself."

I'll say this now and I'll always firmly believe that Art was some sort of a prophet for the music. There's no question about it. I mean, you look at what he did while he was here and he really kind of embodied the perpetuation of the music. I mean, that's really something he represented, and that's a force that he fulfilled, he personified — as a musician and as a spirit. Wherever he was, whatever bandstand he set foot on, there was music, not just great drumming, but something a little more special than that.

Johnny O'Neal introduced me to Art at the Jazz Forum; I had been in town for a few months. He said, "Art, this is Benny Green, a pianist," and Art's eyes lit up the way they always did when he saw some new fresh young blood. And he looked me up and down and said, "How long have you been in New York?" It was the first thing he said to me, and I said (whatever the answer was) "Two months." And he paused for a minute, almost for drama, and he said, "You need more time."

CEDAR WALTON

PIANO; October 1961–April 1964

I used to think that humility was something honorable and Art said "No, that's not right Cedar, you need to be arrogant." What he meant was you need to be confident and exhibit confidence on stage. And I said, well Clifford Brown wasn't arrogant and he said "Yes he was, goddammit!" So he was very emphatic about that, which I think in the long run changed me; I was a stubborn like, a "do unto others" guy, which I think Art was too, but he was trying to teach us that doesn't work on stage. I think that had a tremendous value and a lasting impression on me. It probably filtered into my playing too but it was my playing plus this kind of attitude that was necessary, I think, to be a good jazz performer. That would be one of the most valuable things I got from him.

I was a more timid player when I went in than when I came out. Art was a very gentle encourager … about the most absolute accompanist you can imagine … for both horns and piano because I collaborated with him in the accompaniment of the horns. That's a little different point of view I would have. And he did say things like that to horn players ("Get up outta that hole"). But behind the piano he would come way down especially on the "Theme." That's when I could … after all that, you know he would turn me loose (or whoever was on piano). And you really felt like playin' by that time because you had gone through a whole set of accompaniment and excitement and finally the whole thing is given to you. We had little inserts and that became a tune in itself, but we knew that was the last tune of the set but I was the only solo, you know where the piano was featured. It was very exciting.

JOHN RAMSAY: *When I asked Cedar about the intense level of excitement on the "Free For All" recording session, he had this to say:*

It probably was John, but they all run together for me — they all were exciting. Quite frankly, I guess maybe the material maybe that particular piece ("Free For All") was geared for that kind of open playing by Art.

When I suggested that Art seemed to be changing his style during the time of that recording Cedar said: He tried but Art's style was unchangeable. He probably tried to play bossa-nova or whatever but he was Art — you know, he was his own man. Of course exactly like you said, trying to change his … or trying to update probably just as any conscious musician would. But his style was established. He was an original.

CHARLES FAMBROUGH

BASS; May 1980–May 1982

He (Art) was on my case a lot. The thing he would tell me the most would be slow down and relax, because I played on top of the beat and real forceful. But see I didn't know what he meant — it took me years to figure it out. It's like, what he meant by relax was relax the tension in your attitude not so much the time, but he wasn't talking about the time — he was talkin' about how you apply yourself to the music. He would just say "Calm down! Slow down, the shit ain't goin' nowhere. The shit was here before you got here, it'll be here after you've gone."

When I first joined the band he told me to listen to his bass drum because he was gonna play my parts on his bass drum. And listen to … that he would play the feel of where I should be playing the notes. So the whole first week I played … the first gig I had was in Chicago at The Jazz Showcase, the first week in addition to the other shit, the charts, but he was the one to actually show me where to put the notes with his bass drum. But you know he didn't really need a bass player. I mean he could drown out a bass player with his bass drum. He didn't do that with me because he liked the way I played but if he didn't like the way you played he would run over your ass! He was playing every rhythm that I should have been playing on the bass — he was playing 4/4 too, and the breaks.

So those things kinda locked me into the gig. Consequently I learned how to play with him by listening to his bass drum. So I was never really lost no matter what he played up top. He always kept me hooked up with the bass drum.

JAVON JACKSON

TENOR SAXOPHONE; January 1987–October 1990

I do remember one time Bu was talkin' to me and we were talkin' about individuals and I was talkin' about: wow! you know Sonny Rollins is so great and what he did say to me was, "Hey man, never mind

Sonny Rollins, if you put your thing, whatever your particular perspective of your instrument … your expression on the highest possible level people will recognize it. In other words, you don't have to be like anybody else. And you know, Art didn't want you to sound like anybody(else) He wanted the shit to be different and for it to swing, that's one thing … after that I remember those kinds of things changing my life — in other words, be your own man and don't walk behind any other man. But that's one thing I think he really instilled in me because now I'm an individual and I don't want to be like anybody.

The first week I was with Bu — you know how you get the feature time, the first couple days I didn't get a feature so finally he gave me this feature and I know he could look on my face and tell I was nervous, so he motioned to me with his stick to come over to him, and he whispered in my ear and he said, "Take no prisoners, there may be no tomorrow." And what I got from that is, hey man, get up there and don't bullshit; that's the thing I learned most from being around him. Every time he got on the bandstand, whether he was sick or whether he was feeling depressed or whatever, he got up there and hit. We played the day that his son died and I know that messed him up, he got up there and played. You know, he used to say that people don't care if you don't feel good, they didn't pay for that. So you have to put all that shit aside and the bandstand is hallowed ground.

Curtis Fuller

TROMBONE; June 1961–December 1964
December 1967–December 1968

Some things bothered him (Art) in a way, but he understood where I was coming from. I never liked to play real long solos. I had a joke about it once with Coltrane. I left the club and went to another club and came back. I was only there visiting him, this is when he first put the quartet together because we had a sextet together, Elvin and all of them … and I remember they were playing "Poor Little Inchworm" and I went all the way from the Village Gate to the Five Spot and came back and they were playing the same song. Art used to hate that, you know.

Well, Wayne Shorter used to play like that. But you see saxophone players could do that because they would take ten choruses; but that doesn't sound cool with the trombone doing anything like that; in fact it gets monotonous.

I like to temper what I'm playing, say what I have to say and get the hell out of the way. One

night he got real mad and he told Wayne and Freddie, because they were both long-winded. So he used to refer to me going out and playing first because I'd say what I had to say and get the hell out of the way. And he would get behind them and talk like, "Dig a grave. You're diggin' a hole," and stuff like that. But in other words, he taught me almost something like Basie, you know you edit what you're playing, you say what you have to say. Nobody has that much to play, you start repeating yourself and to you or the audience you get those crowd-pleasers and get a few little licks or some guys hit high notes and everybody screams and they figure, well I gotta do that ten more times.

But he was very … 'cause you know it wears the rhythm section out. He'd say, "Get out of that hole; you're diggin' your own grave." Then he'd go into that press roll and when he did that it wasn't so much … I mean when he was feelin' a lull in your solo that was his way of shifting gears for you.

He helped me to edit and if he felt he was trying to peak he would suggest it with his left hand and the sock cymbal, changing the sock cymbal un-chic-chic un-chic-chic, you know, tiring tempos, that's a suggestion, all right come on now you been foolin' around long enough. In other words, you're boring *me*, now!

Everybody wants to hit paydirt but we forget, like something Lester Young told me and Billie Holiday, "You're talking to people." Because the drum is the heartbeat and if you went into arrhythmia on somebody with your heart or if it went into arrhythmia on you it would rough you up a bit.

Benny Golson

TENOR SAXOPHONE; March 1958–April 1959

Well, that thing sticks out in my mind because that helped me to change my thinking about the way I was playing and I never played that way anymore once I got it together. It wasn't a long tone, it was a whole style — I was playing very mellow and smooth and flowing and it really had no place in his style. See, I was subbing that night and then it turned out I finished the week out see, so he … one night he probably wouldn't have said anything because I wasn't going to be there and the second night he wouldn't say anything, but by the end of the week well, — and I had quite a few nights under my belt — I guess he figured, I better help this boy out, so he played one of those rolls and I disappeared. And then he came down and crashed on the cymbal and said, "Get up outta that hole!" And I heard him say that and I said Darn! maybe I am in a hole. And I started my whole thinking to change to play a little more aggressively and to play out and not so sugary, you know? And that's when it happened with him.

WYNTON MARSALIS

TRUMPET; May 1980–May 1981

He would always tell me it's important to know how to pace a solo. He said, you know, "Just listen to what I'm playing and when I put that bass drum in your ass, that means it's time for you to start reaching for something." And he would say if you're going to play a ballad you have to learn the words to it. I remember how he told me that, he said [in Art Blakey voice] "Who do you think you are, Clifford Brown, mother. . . . er ?"

He also would tell me about playing with intensity, saying that every time you play you have to rededicate yourself to playing like that whenever you play.

JOHN RAMSAY: *You mean like on any given night?*

Every night has got to be the same. Like he would say that by saying "I'm a hundred years old and you're fifteen, [he would exaggerate the years] and I'm out here swinging and you're out here bullshittin'. "

He also told me that you have to learn how to accept who you are. That's the greatest thing he ever told me. This was after I left the band and I was getting a lot of publicity and stuff; and I was going though some changes and he could tell that. He said "You have to accept who you are because other people don't determine their involvement with music, God does." He said "So you never know why, or who's chosen to move the music forward or to have that type of intimate relationship with it. But if it's you, just be grateful and accept it; and don't worry about other people messin' with you or being jealous, that's part of you."

That sounds like something that really had an impact on you.

Yeah, that put me more at ease because at that time I was always questioning whether I actually had a right to play, or whether I could play. He would say if you couldn't play you wouldn't be the one out here playing. But that comes from God; it's not given by a person or a man, and there's nothing anybody can do about it, even you.

You know Buhaina had a very serious spiritual side to him; well you know that.

Yeah, that was the thing that was kind of like what you're talking about; he could always seem to perceive what was going on inside and he would sometimes tell you things that would address whatever conflict was happening or spiritual thing that was going on. I remember another time we were going up the elevator in the Blackstone Hotel in Chicago and I was getting tired of the mess of road manager and Broski throwing soda cans and bouncing them off my head and shit, and I said "Art I need to go, I need to go back to playing, I wanna play." And he was in the elevator with some of his old cronies from Chicago from way back and he said, "John, stay right where you are. The important thing is that you have the knowledge and that you get the information." And that was it man, I think after he said that, it hooked me for another year or so as the road manager. It sounds like the kind of thing you're talking about where he goes right to your personal spiritual center.

Yeah, he knew how to get to the soul. He had that divine connection. It's like what we call divine intelligence, it's something that's beyond thought. It's a region of awareness; he got to that through music. But you can get to it through anything that you do. If you are a deep enough craftsman, and if you have a deep enough belief in faith. Also that's the main thing I learned from Buhaina: faith and belief and the real true meaning of integrity. That's the thing that he had, as much as any man, more than any man that I've known. I'd have to say more than any man that I've known in my entire life. I'd have to say that is what he possessed in abundance. All the things and shit that he could do, none of that meant anything just because of that level of integrity. It's something that's unshakable, and more than it being something in words it would be things that you would learn through gestures, gesture from his soul, soul gestures.

Can you give me any examples?

Man, just Buhaina; he loved musicians. Like if you needed something and he had it, he would give it to you.

And the greatest example would be in the way that he swung every night, providing all that hard, hot swing for musicians who couldn't swing — trading his freedom in so they could be free. That's like the greatest thing any citizen can do; like you know, why should he wanna play with me, man? He played with Clifford Brown, Lee Morgan, people who could play. But he was always out there giving cats who couldn't play the opportunity to learn how to play at his expense; you know what I mean? Because we couldn't play with him, but we didn't even know what the swing was.

That sounds like his commitment to really keeping the music forward and alive.

But you see it's more than that. It's more than his commitment to keeping the music alive. It's his commitment to keeping … it's not even a thing about music, it's a spiritual thing, it's about democracy. That's really where he got it from. It wasn't really about music you know, when you talked with Buhaina, very seldom would he talk about music.

Like a person whose thing is about music would be like a teacher in a college. Every time you see them they talk about a chord or something specific — a technical aspect of music. Whereas when you were with Buhaina, very seldom did he ever touch on the technical aspect of music.

He didn't relate to music that way, because his technique was so refined and so perfectly his, because it came from that region where that divine intelligence is. It had everything in it already; so he would only communicate that type of basic spiritual information about this music. And that information is not even in music, it's about life and about humanity.

And just to watch him as an old man traveling the same road with us, staying in the same places we stayed, doing the same stuff we did and out doing us. Man, I was seventeen, eighteen, and he had more stamina than me. Damn!

I mean, he wanted to swing, but another thing about Buhaina too is this: unlike other people like him, he knew when to give up power. He wasn't the kind of person … he would let somebody run the band.

Like a lot of cats, the few who would be on this level, they would have a problem giving up power. He believed in the freedom of another person. He wasn't gonna try to control you. You know if you wanted to do something else that was fine with him. He could accept that.

He let me run the business; that always amazed me, that he would say "John, go get the money from the club owners," and I would go and get $8,000 sometimes, and I'm thinking to myself, why does he trust me to go and do this stuff? And then he wouldn't ask for it; he would let me hold it. And then sometime later he'd say "Give me some money."

Well his relationship to the world wasn't material. You know, he didn't live in that world. He lived in another world. He was born to swing.

And if you're really playin' from the heart, people can see clean through you — especially children. And whatever is in your heart will come out on the bandstand if you're playing music — especially jazz.

ART BLAKEY

photo: Joji Sawa

Art Blakey's Jazz Messages

Designed and typeset by William R. Brinkley.

The text face is Minion; heads and example text are Gill Sans; the music face is Petrucci.

The music was typeset using Finale® by Coda Music Software; pages composed using QuarkXPress®.

Printed and bound by CPP/Belwin, Inc.